City Slicker
Tyneside

Trevor Hopkins

A guide to sixteen mainly off road cycling routes for all abilities in and around the Tyneside area.

Produced and published by **City Slicker** *Publications*
Fenham, Newcastle upon Tyne

.

Text, Maps, and Design by Trevor Hopkins

ISBN 0 9525593 0 7

Typeset and Printed by Sovereign Press, Felling, Gateshead.

Contents

Photographs

Front Cover: 'City Slickers', Tyne Bridge from the riverside. (Routes 2 & 3) GT Tequesta, GT Timberline bikes and GT Team clothing by GT Bicycles Inc. (UK Distributor Caratti Sports Ltd.) Lent by Derwent Valley Bikes, 38 Front Street, Whickham, Gateshead.
Photograph by Allan Glenwright.

Rear Cover: Resting by 'The Victorian Baker's Shop'.
Stoneware sculpture by Neil Talbot, Felling, Gateshead. (close to Route 3)

'City Slickers'	Routes 2 & 3	page 13
Winter sunset at the Quayside	Routes 2 & 3	page 17
The riverside opposite St Peters	Route 3	page 21
High Gosforth Park	Route 4	page 25
'Marking the Ways' sculpture	Route 10	page 33
Landing lights at Newcastle Airport	Link Route 1	page 37
Crossing a ford in Walbottle Dene	Route 9	page 45
The climb into Heddon	Route 12	page 54

Location Map

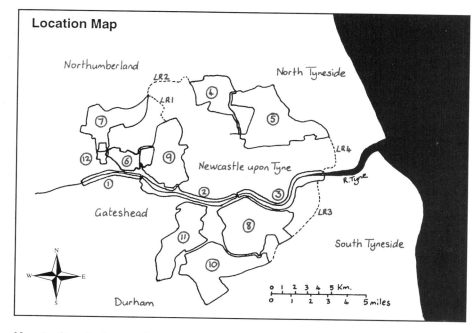

Key to Symbols used on Route Maps

road / bridleway / cycleway		dual carriageway	
roundabout		bridge over / under	
footpath		route	
alternative route		S/F start / finish	
railway line		railway / Metro station	
river		pond	
stream		buildings	
local council boundaries			

Abbreviations used in Route Descriptions

TR	Turn Right	(#?)	Joins or crosses numbered route
TL	Turn Left	(Link#?)	Joins or crosses a link route
R	Right	(R)	Found on your right
L	Left	(L)	Found on your left
SO	Straight On	(T)	Trunk or major road

The routes and maps in this guide are no evidence of the existence of a right of way.
The publishers cannot be held responsible for any omissions, accidents or injuries arising from
following the routes suggested in this guide.

4

Introduction

As a child in the '50s and '60s I remember cycling all over Tyneside on quiet roads. Later in the '70s my wife and I enjoyed several cycle touring holidays in Britain. As our own children grow up in the '80s and '90s the roads round our urban home are unsuitable for safe cycling. The only guides were for experienced mountain bikers or the mostly linear paths set up by local authorities. I began to look for suitable circular off-road routes that were accessible to city dwellers and visitors. It soon became obvious that there was a number of accessible, interesting and challenging circuits. From this came the idea for a guide.

I have tried, where possible, to link the routes with existing cycleways. If you are in Tyneside several tours should be accessible from your front door. You can join at any point and return to your starting place. For drivers, the recommended starts all have parking, most have other facilities. Many of the circuits cross each other making longer excursions possible. Where they do not join up I have suggested link routes. For the adventurous many other combinations are possible.

I have attempted to be as accurate as possible but things change quickly in urban areas. At the time of writing several bypass and reclaimation projects are being planned. Some will enhance these routes, others you may have to cycle round. The main thing is that you get out and enjoy the unique pleasure of cycling in the varied and historically rich environment which Tyneside has to offer.

Acknowledgements

In researching and producing this guide I have been assisted by staff from Durham, Gateshead, Newcastle, North Tyneside, Northumberland and South Tyneside Councils, the Great North Forest and the Tyne and Wear Development Corporation. This book could not have been produced without their support. In addition I am indebted to Courtaulds Coatings for their financial support. I am grateful to Newcastle Racecourse Executive, High Gosforth Park Ltd. and Mr E Lee for permission to use Gosforth Park and Coppy Lane in this guide and J M Clark & Partners for their advice on 'The Winning'.

In particular I would like to thank Alison Bates, Julie and Dave Batra, Kevin Coates, John, Carol and Andrew Earl, Simon Graham, Sue, Dave, Alice and Jenny Hawley, Norman Hopkins, Tony Hopkins, Alan Jessup, Zoe Robson, David, Nicola and Paul Rundle, Ted Sarmiento, Ian Smith and Michael Whittaker for their encouragement, advice and support. My thanks are to them and to Karen, Peter and Zoe who have been at my side, both on and off their bikes, as I compiled this guide.

Useful Contacts

Countryside Commission	Publications and advice	0191 232 8520
Cyclists Touring Club	Routes, outings and support	0191 273 8042
Durham County Council	Routes, advice and information	0191 383 4144
Gateshead Council	Routes, advice and information	0191 477 1011
Great North Forest	Routes, advice and information	0191 410 9066
Newcastle City Council	Routes, advice and information	0191 232 8520
North Tyneside Council	Routes, advice and information	0191 201 0033
Northumberland County Council	Routes, advice and information	01670 533 000
South Tyneside Council	Routes, advice and information	0191 427 1717
Sustrans	Routes, advice and information	01207 281 259
Tyne & Wear Development Corporation	Routes, advice and information	0191 226 1234
Tyne Bikes	Campaign for Cycling Facilities	0191 266 2327

The Bike

So much rubbish is talked about bikes that many people end up buying totally inappropriate bikes for their needs. If you intend to cycle occasionally at weekends then spending hundreds of pounds on a top of the range machine would be a waste of money, unless you just get a thrill possessing such a thing! Equally the 'bargains' at discount stores and hypermarkets may not represent good value for money either.

To attempt most of the routes in this book you will need either a mountain or cross/hybrid bike. Shop around before you buy. Go to specialist cycle shops. Many of their staff are cyclists. Take their advice, remembering that they still want to sell you a bike. It is worth sacrificing fancy accessories for the best frame, wheels, brakes and gears you can afford.

If you don't mind last year's colour or a few chips in the paintwork then a secondhand bike can be the best value for money of all. I did hundreds of miles researching this book on a secondhand bike which I bought and did up for under £65. Take a friend who knows something about bikes. Have a test ride. Worn cables, brake blocks and chains are cheap to replace; frames, gears and wheels are not.

Maintenance

A properly maintained bike will not only last longer but it will be safer and easier to ride. The most basic tasks are cleaning and lubrication. These should be done as often as possible, especially after riding in very wet or muddy conditions.

Bikes are simple pieces of machinery. Unless you like walking and pushing your bike you should at least know how to repair a puncture, adjust your brakes and put the chain back over the cogs. The other tasks involved in keeping your bike running well are easy to master. Buy a good book or ask your cycling friend for lessons. If you absolutely refuse to get your hands dirty then get a cycle shop to service your bike regularly. Your life may depend on it.

Accessories

Many accessories are unnecessary. The more you carry the heavier you and your bike will be. The essentials listed below should be as strong, light and reliable as possible.

Tools

I always carry a small tool kit, even on short journeys. Mine comprises: set of small spanners (or multi tool), tyre levers, set of allen keys, puncture repair kit, chain splitter, piece of soft wire, small adjustable spanner, a reversible phillips/flat screwdriver and a cloth.

First Aid Kit

Carry at least some surgical tape, a few sticking plasters, antiseptic wipes and 'Melolin' pads.

Seat Bag

The above, plus a spare inner tube, should all fit into an expanding wedge seat bag.

Pump

I prefer these to compressed air cylinders for their simplicity and reliability. There are several good mini-pumps available. Those with a 'double action' are more efficient. Get one with clips that fit onto your frame and don't forget a 'velcro' strap to stop it flying off on bumpier descents.

Toe Clips and Straps

If you fit one other accessory other than the above, fit these. They nearly double your pedalling efficiency. If you are worried about getting your feet out quickly, although this should not be a problem with smooth soled shoes, buy strapless toe cups which are nearly as good.

Water Bottle
Most bikes have bottle cages or 'braze-on' lugs to fit them. They are the easiest way to carry a drink. The choice of flavour is up to you.

Lights
If you ride on a public highway after lighting up time you must have front and rear lights and reflectors. There are many lightweight battery models which clip on and off easily. Get ones that meet the current British Standard (BS6102/3). Flashing LEDs are currently illegal as your main light, but they do make eye catching secondary lights.

Cycle Computers
Models of varying sophistication keep track of your time, distance, cadence and speed while touring or training. Not necessary but they can add to the enjoyment of the ride, especially for the more competitive. Heart rate monitors are for serious training only.

Mudguards
Not essential, although they offer some protection in very wet conditions they can become clogged with mud when off road. There are lightweight clip-on plastic models which fit quickly without tools.

Clothing
Personal style aside, there are a few other considerations before choosing your cycling outfit. The climate in the north east can change very rapidly. I remember cycling into the Tyne Pedestrian Tunnel one summer afternoon and coming out the other end in the middle of winter!
The secret is to dress in lightweight layers which trap insulating air but let perspiration through. Outdoor clothing manufacturers and some department stores have developed extensive ranges just for this purpose. There is a bewildering selection of thermal, fleece, wicking and breathable garments for you to try. Hopefully your only problem will be choosing the least frightening colour combination.
Most cyclists recommend wearing proper cycling shorts. They are good but expensive. I must admit to not liking them. An alternative is to buy the padded underwear designed to wear under your own shorts or longs. You don't have to spend a fortune on specialist clothing as long as you follow the principle of dressing in layers using light cotton or woollen fabrics.
Cycling gloves with padded palms add to your comfort and protection. In cold weather they can be worn over thermal gloves or under mitts. Glasses protect eyes against wind, sun, grit and the occasional tree branch. Mine have three interchangable lenses and I wouldn't be without them. You don't need special cycling shoes but avoid boots with high ankle padding. Flat soles are best, especially if you use toe clips.

Safety
Always carry some form of identification just in case of an accident or illness. Any special medical information should also be noted down. I also take a couple of 20p pieces for emergency telephone calls.
Before you start your journey tell someone your time of departure, route, destination and estimated time of arrival or return to base. Remember to let them know when your journey is completed or if you change your plans.
Finally, always wear a helmet. There seems to be those amongst us who have constructed all sorts of arguments as to why cyclists should not wear a helmet. They are idiots, ignore them. Buy a good quality lightweight shell helmet and wear it!

'City Slicking'

In general the skills required to ride a bike can be translated to any environment. Safe steering, braking and the efficient use of gears are developed with practice and experience. However 'City Slickers' need to refine a few additional skills and be aware of certain hazards not regularly encountered on rural routes.

Motor Vehicles

Riding a bike in traffic is dangerous. Obtain and read a copy of the Highway Code. Young children should go on a 'Cycling Proficiency' course run by your local authority. Richard Ballantine in his excellent 'Richard's Bicycle Book' devotes section to 'harassment' by motor vehicles. I make no apologies for listing his main points.

Be alert, be definite, be defensive and expect the unexpected. Keep your hands on or near the brakes at all times. Look for openings in driveways, streets, garages etc. where you can duck into should the need arise. Try to keep moving with traffic and avoid excessive use of your brakes. Always be in a low enough gear to accelerate out of trouble. Don't follow too closely behind cars. Be extra careful at junctions, roundabouts, overtaking parked cars and on multi-lane roads.

Falling Off

This is easy to do, but not properly. It is worth practising skids and falls on a safe loose surface just to get the feel of what will happen. Be extra careful on wet or oily roads, cobblestones and wet leaves. Watch out for broken glass, pot-holes, storm drains and raised manhole covers. If the worst happens try to make the best of a bad situation. The experts' advice is to stay as relaxed as possible, go with the fall and try to roll on impact. Check you and your bike for damage before resuming your journey.

Off Road

One of the main problems encountered on urban tracks is off-road motorcycles. If one hits you your legal position may be unclear, most are unlicensed and uninsured. However they are very noisy so you can usually take early avoiding action. Another hazard is the rubbish people dump on the nearest open space. Builders' rubble, supermarket trolleys, traffic cones, abandoned kitchen appliances, all can damage you if you hit them at speed.

Pedestrians

Because you are quiet and relatively small, pedestrians may not hear or see you coming. A polite but loud shout is often enough. Kids can be unpredictable, especially when playing in suburban streets. Some persons seem to get amusement from challenging cyclists. I can cope with taunts, but if you feel threatened then make a dignified but hasty retreat. It would take a determined effort to outrun the average cyclist.

Dogs

Richard Ballantine's theory, that 'the spokes make a noise which drives them nuts' may not be scientifically accurate but I sympathise with his sentiments. All dogs must be regarded as potential enemies to cyclists. Slow down and give them a wide berth. If an attack looks imminent the best strategy is to stop, dismount and walk past, speaking firmly to the creature. Keep the bike between yourself and it. If an attack comes then defend yourself with anything that comes to hand: a large rock, your helmet, the cycle pump or the bike itself.

Manufacturers of puncture repair kits would sell their souls for an adhesive that squeezes out of a small tube, stays fluid then immediately sticks to the rubber tread of a bicycle tyre on contact. Such a substance is freely deposited over most cycleways by our friend the dog. The only answer, I'm afraid, is a bucket, a bottle of disinfectant and a scrubbing brush. Keep a set of these at home, just for this purpose, don't use your household equipment.

Types of Rights of Way

A very good booklet on your rights and responsibilities called 'Out In The Country' is available from: Countryside Commission Postal Sales, PO Box 124, Walgrave, Northampton, NN6 9TL, Telephone 01604 781848. The following information, taken from this publication, is intended only for guidance and information. The only up-to-date and legal source on rights of way in your area is the definitive map and accompanying statement. These have to be prepared and updated by the county or metropolitan council responsible for the area concerned. You have a right to see both the map and the statement in order to check the status of rights of way.

Footpaths
A footpath may be used only for walking. Strictly speaking you must carry your bike, but I'm sure you can push without any problems. A few of the routes in this guide cross footpaths, mainly on bridges and in underpasses.

Bridleways
These may be used for walking, riding and cycling. Cyclists must give way to walkers and riders. Driving a vehicle is not permitted, even if it is horse-drawn.

Byways
This is a highway that is used mainly for walking, riding horses or cycling. There is also a right to use any kind of wheeled vehicle on byways.

Green Lanes
This term has no legal meaning.

Roads Used As Public Paths (RUPPs)
The exact status of these is very ambiguous and they are currently all being reclassified. However you have at least the same rights on a RUPP as on a bridleway.

Public Roads
It is usually safe to assume that that you can drive, walk or ride along those roads and lanes that are shown in colour on Ordnance Survey maps, unless there are clear notices to the contrary. Some minor lanes are shown uncoloured and for this reason they are sometimes known as 'white roads'. It will usually be obvious, either from the map or on the ground, whether a particular lane or track is public or private; for instance if it leads solely to a country house or a farm it will be private. Ask your local council for advice if you are not sure.

Permissive Paths

A landowner may be willing to let you use other paths and tracks over his land that are not public rights of way. These are termed 'permissive paths' which you do not have a statutory right to use. Often there will be a notice at either end of the route explaining this and outlining any conditions that the owner has set.

Maps

The ideal map for the 'City Slicker' does not exist. It would be a cross between an Ordnance Survey map and an 'A to Z'. All the routes in this guide are covered by the Ordnance Survey Landranger sheet 88 'Tyneside & Durham Area', but apart from general route planning it does not show enough detail. The OS Pathfinder series are much better but you would need to carry four with you to cover some of the routes in this guide.

For this reason I have included sketch maps of all the routes. They show the main features of the rides and should be used in conjunction with the route descriptions.

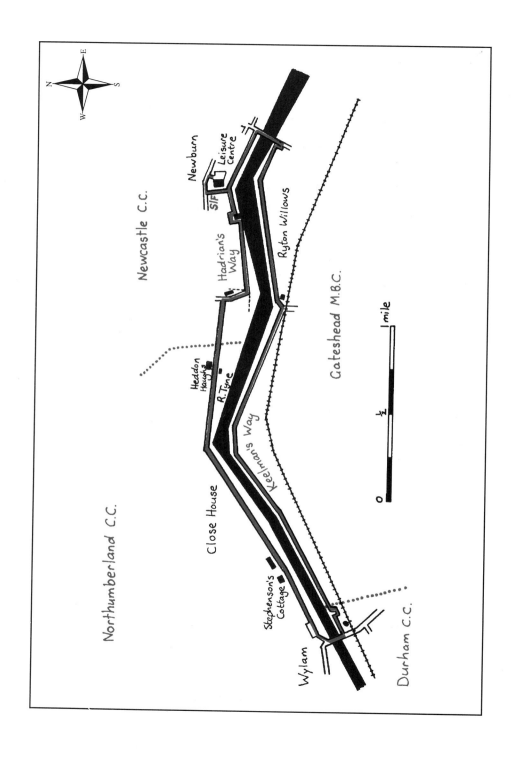

1. Easy Peasy
Riverbank Circuit 1. (Newburn Bridge to Wylam Bridge)

Distance:	7.25 miles (11.7 Km.)
Level:	Very Easy
Maps:	**Ordnance Survey Pathfinder 548 'Blaydon and Prudhoe'**
Facilities:	**Newburn Leisure Centre - toilets, changing, showers, vending machines for snacks and drinks. Picnic area and children's playground at Newburn Riverside Park. Shops, toilets and pubs in Wylam. Toilets, drinks and pub grub at 'The Boathouse'.**
Parking:	**Newburn Leisure Centre or Tyne Riverside Park.**

Introduction

The first and easiest route in this book. Except for the two bridges, it is all off road, on excellent quality cycle paths. The gradients are gentle but there is enough variety of terrain to make it fun to ride. It is quite short and the route is very easy to follow. It is an ideal circuit for complete beginners and groups with young children. I don't think that this ride would be too much for a reasonably fit 6-7 year old in dry and warm conditions.

For a guide which uses disused wagon ways and railway lines in most of its routes, it is apt that the first circuit in this book passes the birthplace of the 'Father of the Railways' George Stephenson born in 1781. The cottage, built around 1750, is owned by the National Trust. There is also a small railway museum in Wylam commemorating the work of George Stephenson and other local railway pioneers.

This, and the other two riverside routes, can be ridden seperately or combined to give rides of 7, 14, 15, 21, 29 and 36 miles.

Route Description

Leave Leisure Centre car park (**#6**). **TL** then **TL** into car park for 'Tyne Riverside Park'. Go **SO** to join the riverside cycle path. **TR** and follow the path with 'River Tyne' (L). **TR**, **TL** and **TL** past 'Newburn Slipway' (L). Continue on path round to **R** with children's playground (R), **SO** through grassy area. As a terrace of houses approaches (R) the path splits into three, take the middle path, signposted 'Wylam Wagon Way' which leads to a gate close to the front of the row of houses. Go through gate and **SO** past houses (R) to join tarmac road. After about 50 metres **TL** over a barrier and onto the 'Wylam Wagon Way'.

SO through gate, farm (R) (**#6**) and house (L). Continue **SO** with bushes (L) and fields (R). The way eventually passes 'Close House' (R) with playing fields and a golf course. Continue **SO** past row of stone cottages (R) and 50 metres further on you will pass George Stephenson's birthplace (R). **SO** past farm buildings (R) and glasshouses (L). At the end of the wagon way go through a barrier and **SO** path to parking area ahead. At end of car park **TL**, go through gate, past memorial cross on green (R) and **SO** over 'Wylam Bridge' ahead.

Just before level crossing and footbridge **TL** into station car park. Join the 'Keelman's Way' which is to your **R** at the end of the car park. Go through the barrier by stone wall then **TL** onto the main path. Go **SO** through woods along the riverbank with the river (L). The path eventually emerges at the edge of 'Ryton Golf Course' (R). Continue **SO** until the path goes uphill, close by railway line (R), to pedestrian railway crossing (R). **TL** downhill on tarmac road with large white residence (R). Bear **R** towards fence with two gates ahead. Go **SO** through the **L** gate onto 'Ryton Willows' countryside park. Continue **SO** very close to river now (L). Go **SO** through second gate and under power lines. **SO** to 'Newburn Bridge' ahead and under second set of power lines. Just before the bridge **TR** through gate and go up steep ramp to road. (**#2**) **TL** and go over the bridge.

At the far end of the bridge **TL** downhill on tarmac lane past 'The Boathouse' public house (R). Go through gate and **SO** with electricity pylon ahead.

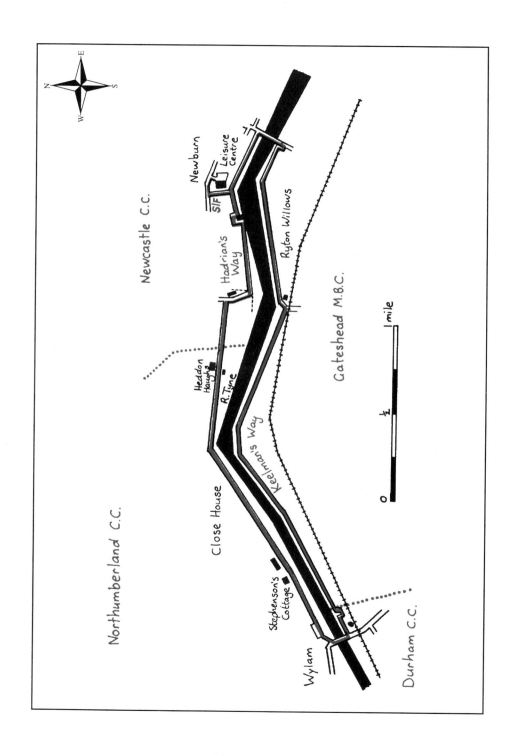

Take fork to **L** and pass pylon (**R**). Follow playing fields round to **R**, **TL** to cross stream on footbridge then **TR** into car park. **SO** to road then **TR** (#6) and **TR** again into Centre car park and finish.

 City of Newcastle upon Tyne

Cycling in the City of Newcastle

For many years Newcastle City Council has been promoting existing and new routes out into the countryside. New cycle routes have been largely on Council owned land. These include the Havannah Local Nature Reserve near Hazlerigg, along disused wagon ways around Percy Pit and in Newbiggin Dene. Some gaps in the network still exist where land is privately owned.

The flagship recreational route is now nearing completion along the north bank of the River Tyne. Previously known as the North Tyne Cycleway, the Hadrian's Way is now part of the Hadrian's Wall National Trail. Created in conjunction with the Tyne & Wear Development Corporation and the Countryside Commision, it passes through the heart of Tyneside, but is almost entirely traffic free.

The Council recognises that cycling is not just for recreation and is now making provision for the cyclist around town. Safe routes from the Coast Road via Heaton and from Haddricksmill via Jesmond, both to the City Centre, have been signed. On the latter route is Newcastle's first Toucan light controlled pedestrian/cycle crossing at Jesmond Dene Road. The problems of City Centre cycling are being studied and major new schemes such as the West Central Route are designed with the cyclist in mind. The best source of information on advisory routes in Newcastle is the 'Countryside Strategy and Guide' available from libraries.

There are routes in Newcastle on pages: 11, 15, 19, 23, 27, 31, 43, 56 & 57.

For further information contact:

Development Department, Newcastle City Council, Civic Centre, Barras Bridge, Newcastle upon Tyne, NE1 8PH.
Telephone. (0191) 232 8520. ext. 5637

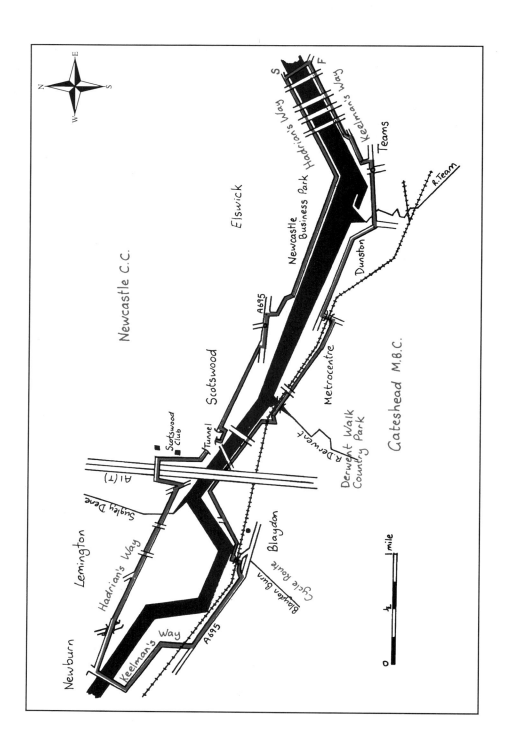

2. Lemon Squeezy

Riverbank Circuit 2. (Swing Bridge to Newburn Bridge)

Distance:	14.0 miles (22.5 Km.)
Level:	Easy
Maps:	Ordnance Survey Pathfinder 549 'Newcastle upon Tyne'; 548 'Blaydon & Prudhoe'
Facilities:	Cafes, restaurants and pubs on Newcastle quayside. Various pubs and shops on route.
Parking:	Meter, ticket and free parking on both sides of the quayside.

Introduction

This is the second circuit based on Newcastle and Gateshead's riverside cycle ways. It also includes areas recently regenerated by the Tyne & Wear Development Corporation. Unlike the previous route it includes some road sections. I am no fan of mixing it with motor vehicles but the roads are just bearable if you avoid weekday mornings and late afternoons. We usually let the kids ride on the pavement alongside the busier main roads. Strictly speaking it is against the law, but as long as they ride carefully and give way to pedestrians I can see no real problem. Some pavements and underpasses are shared or have marked off lanes for cyclists. Not the ideal solution, but better than nothing at all.

This route with a mix of cycle paths, reclaimed railway lines, tracks, bridleways and roads gives beginners to 'City Slicking' an excellent introduction to the types of routes they will find in the rest of this book. Look out for some good views of the river, especially opposite Dunston Staithes. There are sculptures on both riverside paths. My favourite is 'Rolling Moon' by Colin Rose, close to the Tyne Bridge on the South Bank. Would it be too romantic to see the shining steel arc amongst the trees as an image close to the hearts of off-road cyclists?

Route Description

Follow paved path under 'Swing Bridge' and 'High Level Bridge' with 'River Tyne (L). Continue under the three bridges on riverside path. Past business park (R) go through car park then uphill to **R**, join road and continue **R** to traffic lights with 'The Armstrong' public house (R). **TL** and continue **SO** over roundabout. After 100 metres cross the main road to the 'Hadrian's Cycleway' which goes up to the **L** opposite. **SO** past 'Whitehouse Enterprise Centre' (R) until you are level with 'Scotswood Bridge'. The path forks in three here. The path to the **L** leads to a footbridge. The path ahead leads to a tunnel which has been blocked off. Take the middle path which goes slightly downhill.

TR, **TL** and at the 'Sporting Arms' public house (L) **TR** into subway. **TL** through tunnel and go uphill at end. **SO** past 'Scotswood Social Club' (R). **TL** at fork (**SO #9**) and keep **L** through playing fields to footbridge over A1(T). Cross bridge and **TL** at end. Follow path down through grassed area and gate to road. Cross road then **TR** uphill on cycle path which bears off to **L** and across 'Sugley Dene'. Continue **SO** cyclepath through a series of barriers and under bridges. At fork in the path **TL** and **SO** to T junction with road. (**#1** and **SO#6**)

TL over 'Newburn Bridge' and continue **SO**. Follow this road **L** then **R**, **TL** and follow this over railway crossing and **SO** uphill to main road. **TL** and follow this road. Just after the sign for Blaydon, with Coffee Centre (R) **TL** down track to 'Blaydon Burn'. **TL** at the big stones, under the railway line then **TR** along the river bank. **SO** past 'Blaydon Station' (R) to 'Blaydon Haughs Industrial Estate'. **TL** into 'Factory Road'. **SO** into 'Patterson Street' to river then **TR** onto the 'Keelman's Way'. **SO** along the riverside under bridges. Past the marina **TR** and cross the railway. **TL** past 'The Skiff' public house (L) and take path to cross the 'River Derwent' by railway bridge. (**#11**) Keep on twisty path, under road, past station (L) and 'Metrocentre' (R). At main road (**#11**) **TL** under bridge then **TR**. **SO** this road past 'The Royal Hotel' and 'Tudor Rose' public houses (L). Go under footbridge with 'River Team' (L) and **TL** signposted 'Low Teams'. (**#8**) **SO** past gas works (R) to roundabout. **SO** into 'Rose Street' and **TL** before the houses onto stony path.

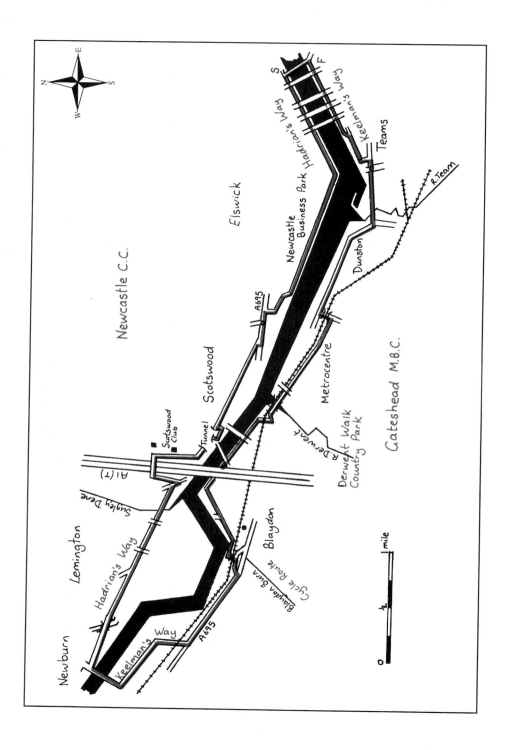

Follow path to **R** and **SO** for a magnificent view of the bridges. Fork to **L** and go downhill under bridges onto road past oil depot (L). **SO** up short hill to junction, **(#3** and **#8) TL** and cross 'Swing Bridge' to finish.

The Tyne and Wear Development Corporation

Tyne and Wear Development Corporation was formed by the Government in 1987 to regenerate the riversides of the Tyne and the Wear, covering four local authorities (North and South Tyneside, Sunderland and Newcastle) with over 30 miles of riverbank. They have already brought £750 million investment into the region and should hit £1 billion when they complete their task in 1998.

They are working on or have completed over 20 projects including Newcastle Business Park, St Peter's Basin, North Shields Fish Quay, and are working to complete the flagship projects at Newcastle Quayside, Royal Quays, the Enterprise Park and St Peter's Riverside in Sunderland. Their commitment is to total regeneration: physical, in restoring the land to a usable state and providing the infrastructure needed; economic, in bringing significant new investment, expanding local companies and training; social, providing low cost housing and opening up new education opportunities. They are bringing new leisure activities including the Customs House centre in South Shields; encouraging watersports; enabling access for all through design and planning; encouraging the study of heritage through trails and information boards; major public arts provision and maintaining a nature reserve.

All of this is done in partnership, particularly with the local community, and with the other agencies, councils and bodies in the area. This also includes completing the walk/cycleway along the north bank of the Tyne. Enjoy exploring the area and return regularly to see all of its attractions.

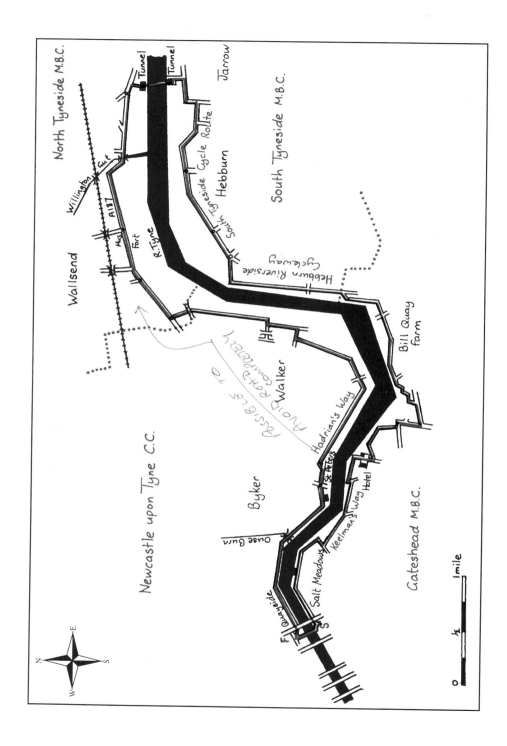

3. The Early Bath
Riverbank Circuit 3. (Swing Bridge to Cycle Tunnel)

Distance:	15.4 miles (24.7 Km.)
Level:	Easy
Maps:	Ordnance Survey Pathfinder 549 'Newcastle upon Tyne'
Facilities:	Pubs and cafes on the quayside. Toilets at Bill Quay, Farm. Pubs and shops on both road sections.
Parking:	Meter, ticket and free parking on both sides of the quayside

Introduction

The longest and most strenuous of the three riverbank circuits, about half is on the 'Keelman's' and 'Hadrian's' cycle ways. Both give magnificent views along the river. Much of the lower Tyne was formerly occupied by shipbuilding. Some of the land, mainly on the north bank, is now being redeveloped. Oil platform construction and ship repair still continue in places but the rest, like many of the shipyard workers, lies redundant and bearing the scars of previous employment. As they come into view on a great bend in the river it is difficult not to feel nostalgic about the cranes and docks of Britain's former industrial heartland.

The eastern half of this route is all on roads and includes the Tyne Pedestrian Tunnel, an experience which just makes the traffic worth bearing. There are plans to develop a disused railway track which runs from behind the Roman fort at Wallsend through Low Walker. I've explored some of it but other bits are currently fenced off. The return path passes the recently developed St Peter's Marina and Newcastle Quayside area. It is particularly impressive at dusk when the floodlit bridges form the centre-piece to one of Tyneside's best known views.

Route Description

Start on the Gateshead side of the 'Swing Bridge'. **(#2 and #8)** Go up the hill and **TL** signposted 'Gateshead East Industrial Estate'. **SO** under the 'Tyne Bridge', past 'Baltic Flour Mill' (L) and ready mixed cement works (L). At end **TR** up short hill then first **TL**, **SO** to end of road and onto riverside path. **SO** downhill and take the path ahead along the riverbank. **TL** downhill, **TR** at the hairpin bend and continue alongside river. At 'Riverside Lodge' hotel **TR** up steep hill and go **SO** through car park. At junction before factory unit **TL** on path right between trees. Follow this path to T junction with road. **TL** and follow road to **R** past main entrance of Courtaulds Coatings (L). Take first **TL** onto 'Abbotsford Road'. Just before the first industrial unit (L) **TL** onto path, follow the path round behind unit and downhill at back of paint works (L). At bottom of the hill go **SO** to join the riverside path again. **SO** path bearing **R** then **L** through a small copse then **SO** with wall (L) and 'Bill Quay Farm' (R) **(#8)** to end where it becomes 'Jonadab Road'. Cross road with 'Albion Inn' (L) and the 'Cricketers' (R) and take gravel path uphill past scrap yard (L). Bear to **L** uphill with wood (L) and **SO** this undulating path with views of the river (L).

The path finally bears to **R** uphill to join the 'South Tyne Cycleway' at a T junction. **TL** onto cycleway and go **SO**. At crossroads continue **SO** uphill then downhill to join road behind 'Hebburn Marina' (L). **SO** road then **TR** uphill past 'Prince Consort Industrial Estate' (L). At roundabout **TL** on the B1297 signposted 'Jarrow'. Continue on this road **SO** over two roundabouts past 'Dougie's Tavern' (R). You will see the inverted cone ventilator shaft for the Tyne Tunnel straight ahead. Follow road to **L** and **R** past industrial park (L) **(TR Link#3)**, the 'Western', 'Rolling Mill' and 'Jarrow Lad' pubs. **TL** at the next roundabout signposted 'Tyne Tunnel A19 South Shields A185' and follow the road round to **R**. Pass ventilator shaft (R) then **TL** downhill past 'The Gas Light' public house (R) to the entrance of the pedestrian/cycle tunnel. **(Links #3 and #4)**

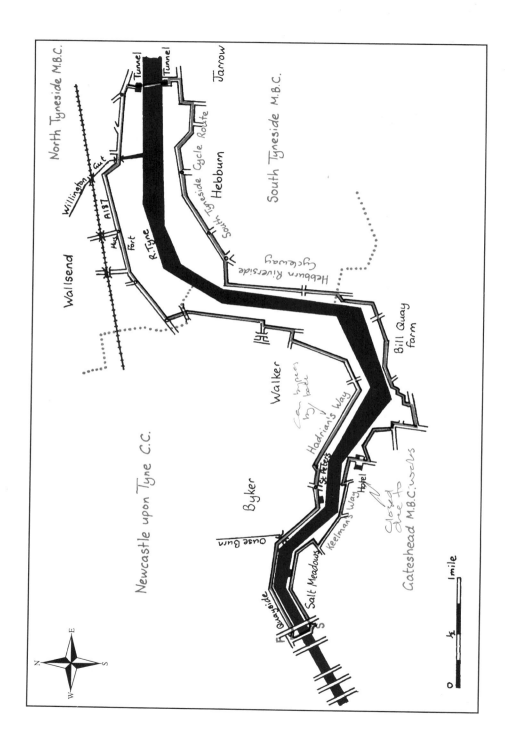

On leaving the north side of the tunnel go uphill to T junction with main road. **(TR Link #4) TL** and go **SO** to roundabout. **TL** on first exit signposted 'Wallsend A187'. Continue **SO** across traffic lights and bear downhill to **R** at 'Willington Gut' where 'Wallsend Burn' joins the 'River Tyne'. Continue uphill bearing to **L** past 'Hadrian Lodge Hotel' (L). **SO** at next roundabout on 'A187' and continue past 'Wallsend Heritage Centre', a small local museum (R) and 'Segedunum' Roman fort (L). Continue **SO** across roundabout and at next roundabout **TL** downhill signposted 'Low Walker'.

Go under **L** side of railway bridge and bear uphill to **R** past terrace of houses (L). **SO** downhill past 'Royal George Hotel' and continue on the main road until it bears round to **R**. Just before it goes under the railway bridge **TL** onto 'Wincomblee Road'. Continue past works (L) and take first **TR** uphill on 'Malaya Drive'. After 50 metres **TL** onto the 'Hadrian's Cycle Way'.

Through barriers go **SO** cycle way with houses (R) and ship repair yard (L). At the fork in the path **TL** and continue to second fork where you **TR** and go **SO** past gasometer (R). Continue downhill and cross road through barriers to continue **SO** cycleway. There are excellent views of the river from this path but watch out for the speed bumps. The cycle way finishes downhill, through a barrier to road.

TR and pass 'Foundry Court' and 'Dobson Crescent' (L) to mini roundabout ahead. Go **SO** downhill to 'Spiller's Flour Mill'. Pass the mill (L) and **TL** across open area with rail lines to paved promenade alongside river. Follow the river as closely as possible heading upstream. This whole area is being redeveloped (early 1995) so the final route may change slightly, but stick to the riverside and the magnificent view of the bridges will soon appear ahead. Continue **SO** under the 'Tyne Bridge' onto a cobbled lane with the circular 'Guildhall' (R). **TR** up narrow cobbled lane, **TL** then **TL** again onto the 'Swing Bridge' and the finish. **(#2)**

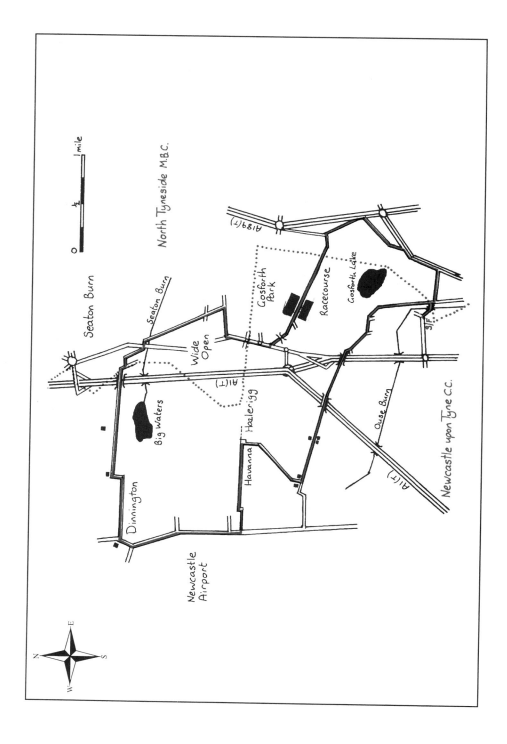

4. Hunter's Handicap

Circuit from Gosforth via Wide Open, Dinnington and Fawdon

Distance:	**13.9 miles (22.4 Km.)**
Level:	**Easy**
Maps:	**Ordnance Survey Pathfinder 536 'Whitley Bay'; 549 'Newcastle upon Tyne'**
Facilities:	**Toilets, drinks and pub grub available at 'Border Minstrel' Gosforth Park. Other pubs on route. Toilets and cafe at 'Barratts Garden Centre' 150 metres beyond Gosforth Park gates.**
Parking:	**Car parking area on Broadway East. Take A189 road north from Newcastle through Gosforth. TR at next roundabout after ASDA supermarket.**

Introduction

I rode the first half of this circuit with my family on New Year's Day 1995. By Gosforth Park we had all fallen off on black ice. My daughter Zoe made a particularly impressive dent in her helmet, which should be a lesson to us all. As we cut back towards home, cold and bruised, the first runners in the annual Morpeth to Newcastle road race were passing. I stopped to watch a few friends go by including the irrepressible Stan Hunter, setting a PB at the age of 58!

This is not the route I originally planned. Between West Bruntoh Farm and Fawdon is a disused mineral line which Newcastle City Council plan to develop as a cycle way. This would give an excellent off road route under the A1 to Gosforth. However as this has not yet happened and the owners of the land will not grant permission for its use, I have had to make an alternative route. Hopefully, by the next edition of 'City Slicker', the problem will be overcome.

Route Description

Leave car park on tarmac bridleway past 'Broadway East First School' (R). **SO** over footbridge at 'Gosforth Golf Club' (R) and past car park (R). **SO** through gate leaving tarmac surface and follow the bridleway through a series of bends then through gate to a T junction. (**#5**) **TR** then almost immediately **TL** onto old road and **SO** to end. At main road **TL** onto dual carriageway for about 800 metres. Just past sign for the roundabout **TL** and **TR**, through gate onto disused road. **SO** up incline to the end of the road. Through the gate **TL** and follow the dual carriageway. You can cycle on the road or the muddy path on the verge.

After 200 metres **TL** onto the slip road signposted 'Gosforth Park 1\4'. Take first **TL** into the park. The road through the park is not a public right of way. The owners are happy for cyclists to use it. Please stick to the route and respect the other users of the facility. As part of a family outing have a day at the horse racing held regularly on the racecourse in the park. Go **SO** this road through woods. Continue past the golf course (R) until you reach the racecourse complex and 'Border Minstrel' public house (L). Just past these buildings do not follow road to L but go **SO** through white metal barred gate and onto downhill section, under bridge and up the other side to park gates with stone gatehouse (R). (**#5**)

At main road **TR** and go **L** at first and **SO** second roundabouts following signs for 'Wide Open B1318'. Pass row of houses (R) and **TR** just after a ruined cottage (R) onto disused railway track signposted 'Greenshouses 11/4'. Take the **R** side path as the L leads to a scrap yard. At T junction with paths (**#5**) **TL**. Continue **SO** this cycle track over crossroads, past fields (R) and backs of houses (L). Cross footbridge over stream and continue to main road. **SO** over road and continue on cycle track opposite. **SO** past back of old painted terrace of houses (L). Go through gate then **TL** downhill past end of terrace (L) and **SO** over footbridge to T junction with paths. **TR** and follow path **L** to bridge over A1(T). Continue **SO** this wide track, through a series of gates. Follow the track round to the **L** and **R** then continue slightly uphill to join tarmac road at Dinnington. **SO** to main road and **TL** (**TR Link#2**) past 'North Mason Farm' (R) on S bend.

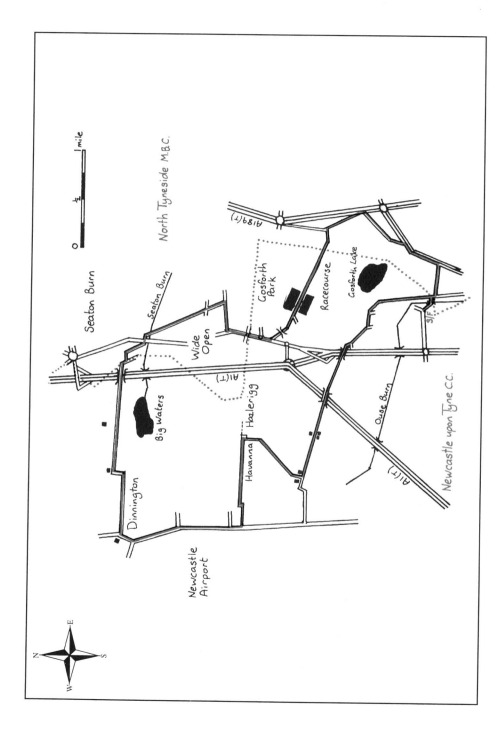

North Tyneside M.B.C.

Seaton Burn

Seaton Burn

A189(T)

Gosforth Park

Racecourse

Gosforth Lake

Wide Open

A1(T)

Havanna

Hazlerigg

Big Waters

Dinnington

Ouse Burn

A1(T)

S/F

Newcastle upon Tyne C.C.

Newcastle Airport

1 mile

N E S W

Go **SO** through village 'Bay Horse' public house (R) and continue out of village past road (L) signposted 'Brunswick, Wide Open' then 'Newcastle Airport' runways (R). **SO** past road (L) signposted 'Hazelrigg, Wide Open and Killingworth' for about 200 metres then **TL** through gate onto paved track.

Continue onto gravel track through fields, **TL** and **TR** round pond then **SO** through gate into plantation of trees. Continue **SO** to tarmac car park. This area is the 'Havanna' nature reserve. **TR** into car park and continue **SO** through gate at top of car park onto a narrow track. As you approach the fields ahead bear to **R** then **SO** through gate on long narrow path between bushes with power lines overhead. At end **TL** onto track through farm to road.

TL onto narrow road past 'Hawthorne Farm' (L) and go **SO** past next farm (R) and detached houses (L & R). Continue over bridge across the A1(T) and **SO** with housing estate (R). Just before the dual carriageway ahead **TR** and, using the footbridge, cross the main road to the opposite side. **TL** back on yourself and after 20 metres **TR** into 'Glamis Avenue'. (**#5**) **TL** at T junction. Go **SO** past four roads to L then road bends to R bear **L** onto 'Kingsley Avenue'. Continue **SO** until this road bears to R and **TL** into 'Ferndale Avenue'. Go **SO** to gate at the end of this street. **TR** onto stony path signposted 'Heathery Lane 2/3'. Follow path through woods and out into open fields.

SO through gate and past stone building (R). Just before path forks by golf course (**#5**) **TR** through gate and follow the bridleway through a series of bends past the golf club car park and club house (L). **SO** over the footbridge and join the tarmac surface past school (L), into the car park and the finish.

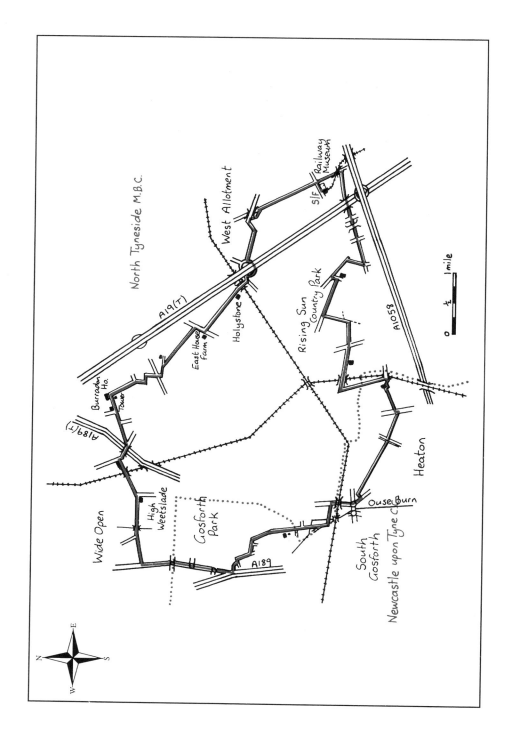

5. Up and Under
Circuit from Wallsend via Wide Open, South Gosforth and Benton

Distance: 17.25 miles (27.75 Km.)

Level: Easy

Maps: Ordnance Survey Pathfinder 549 'Newcastle upon Tyne'; 536 'Whitley Bay'.

Facilities: Toilets at museum. Several pubs and shops on route.

Parking: George Stephenson Railway Museum, Wallsend. Follow signs off A1058(T) 'Coast Road' from Newcastle to Whitley Bay.

Introduction

The industrial history of South Northumberland is dominated by coal mining and the railways. This route starts, crosses and finishes on disused railway lines left from the heydays of steam and 'King Coal'. The grimy black grit which covers these paths once covered the faces and clothes of pitmen cycling home after a shift underground. The spoil heaps at West Allotment, Burradon, High Weetslade and Rising Sun are all still visible.

Along this route there are plenty of allotments where prize vegetables for both show and pot are still grown. At weekends you may still see the traditional whippet racing in the fields nearby. Reminders of the tough existences of the rural and urban working classes are never far away.

As you cycle round you may like to reflect that their lives, work and achievements have passd by, sometimes deep below your wheels. This is the very first route that I mapped for 'City Slicker'. It is an excellent route for a longer family outing. Take a picnic and stop at 'Gosforth' or 'Rising Sun' parks on the way round.

Route Description

Leave the museum car park to road **TR** then **TL** onto disused railway line. (**TR Link#4**) **SO** long straight section then just before the bridge over the track bear to **L** up steep embankment to road. **TL** and take the main road round into 'West Allotment' following signs for 'Gosforth A191' past the 'Northumberland Arms' public house (L). Continue on main road to roundabout under the A19(T). Take the exit for the A191 and immediately cross the road and go up the short hill to the **R** of the 'Holystone' public house. It is signposted 'Public Bridleway East House Farm 11/3 2.25 Km.' **SO** to cross railway line on concrete bridge. Follow bridlepath **SO** through farm buildings to gate ahead. Through this gate the bridlepath is indistinct so follow edge of field (R). After about 200 metres a track appears. Follow this bearing **R** and **L**, through two gates heading for the farm buildings ahead.

At T junction **TR** onto road. Go past road to L then almost immediately **TL** onto public bridleway signposted 'Northgate 11/3 miles'. Go **SO** between bushes to open area with good views north to coast. **SO** through gate past playing fields (L) and into woods. At tarmac road bear to **L** and **SO** to main road. Go across road to public bridleway opposite signposted 'Burradon Tower 1/2 Burradon 3/4'. Follow narrow path at the edge of field round to **L** then **TR** down grassy lane. Join gravelly lane and head **SO** towards farm buildings in trees ahead.

Pass 'Burradon Tower' (L) with row of stone cottages ahead and **TL** uphill through farm to join tarmac road. **SO** past more stone cottages (R) and factory unit (R). **SO** onto main road and pass 'Cheviot Grange' (L). Where road bends to L go **SO** narrow track with field (R). At the bottom of the field **TL** uphill to main road. **TR** and cross A19(T) on bridge. Take next **TL** signposted 'High Weetslade B1319'. **SO** over railway line and where the road bears to L go **SO** past farm (L) onto public bridleway signposted 'Wide Open 11/2'.

Continue **SO** through gates following rough track with spoil heap (R). **SO** over a culvert on little bridge. Where the path forks (#4) **TL** and pass scrap yard (R). Go **SO** through barriers to T junction with main road. **TL** and follow signs for 'Gosforth B1318'

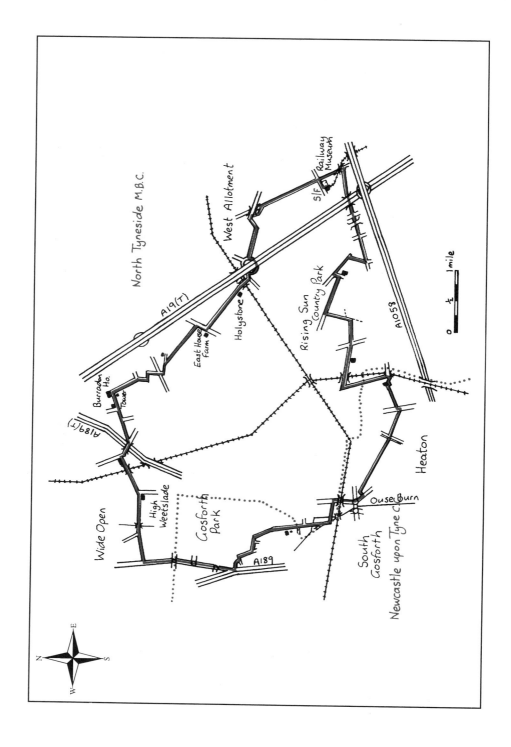

Cycling in North Tyneside

North Tyneside Council is committed to promoting cycling as a healthy, more environmentally friendly form of transport to the motor car. For the last two years the Council has been developing its old waggonways, which are a legacy of the area's long tradition of coal mining, as bridleways and cycle tracks. The aim is to provide a whole range of traffic free routes across North Tyneside and create links to neighbouring areas for residents and visitors. A map and guide entitled 'Pedalling Paths' has been produced to publicise the range of routes available to cyclists. It is available from libraries and tourist information centres. It is hoped that the work carried out on the network will compliment schemes being undertaken by adjoining authorities and the proposed 'North Tyne Cycleway' being established by the Tyne & Wear Development Corporation along the river.

The North Tyneside Cycleway Network is being established in partnership with the Countryside Commission, the Department of the Environment and Sustrans. Emphasis is placed on designing tracks with good surfacing and appropriate access controls to prevent the routes being used by motor cyclists.

It is hoped that this project will encourage people not only to get out and about in the Borough, whether to work, shop or for enjoyment, but also to provide a pleasant way to stay healthy and fit. There are routes in North Tyneside on pages: 19, 23, 27 & 60.

For further information contact:

The Environment Strategy Team, Graham House, Whitley Road, Benton, Newcastle upon Tyne, NE12 9TQ.
Telephone. (0191) 201 0033

Go over three roundabouts and past 'Gosforth Park Racecourse' (L). (#4) Join A189(T) dual carriage way at slip road and just before the footbridge **TL** into 'Glamis Avenue'. (#4) **TL** at T junction. Go **SO** past four roads to L then as the road bends to R bear **L** onto 'Kingsley Avenue'. Continue **SO** until this road bears R and **TL** into 'Ferndale Avenue'. Go **SO** to the gate at end of this street. **TR** onto stony path signposted 'Heathery Lane 2/3'. Follow path through woods and out into open fields. **SO** through gate and past stone building (R). At golf course take **R** fork in path. (#4) **SO** through gates, cross river and **SO** road ahead to T junction. **TL** and follow road round to **L**, over bridge to T junction with A189. **TR** and go under 'Metro' line to roundabout at 'South Gosforth'.

Go **SO** over roundabout then first **TL** up 'Lartington Gardens'. At top of street join 'Coxlodge Wagonway' to **R**. Follow this very straight path uphill and down to cross 'Benton Road'. Pick up track opposite and continue **SO** to 'Coach Lane'. **TL** and immediately **TR** onto old road. **SO** to 'Little Benton Farm'. Follow track **R**, **L**, through farm yard, **R** and **L** towards bridge ahead. Just before bridge **TL** and follow railway line (R). Follow path to **L** and **R** past playing fields (R). At crossroads with entrance to sports centre (R) go **SO**, over railway and past farm (R). Cross road and continue **SO** track signposted 'Rising Sun 3/4'. Go through barrier and **TL** at T junction. Ignore turning uphill (R) and follow drainage ditch (L) past bushes (R). Finish uphill through barrier to T junction. **TR** onto Public Bridleway signposted 'Rising Sun 3/4 1.25 Km.' Go **SO** to 'Rising Sun Farm'. **TL** at T junction. Bear **L** then **SO** to T junction. **TR** onto cycle way. Just before the end **TR** through gate and follow twisting downhill path to barrier and crossroad of paths. **TL** and **SO** path past houses and playing field (R).

Join paved section, cross road 'Addington Drive' and **SO** across grassy area. **SO** across next road and join disused railway track under bridge. Cross next road and **SO** signposted 'Railway Museum 3/4'. Just after the railway track joins (L) **TR** down stony hill and **TL** back on yourself under railway bridge. Continue **SO** uphill on railway track to barrier and road. **TL** and **TL** back into museum car park and finish. (**Link#4**)

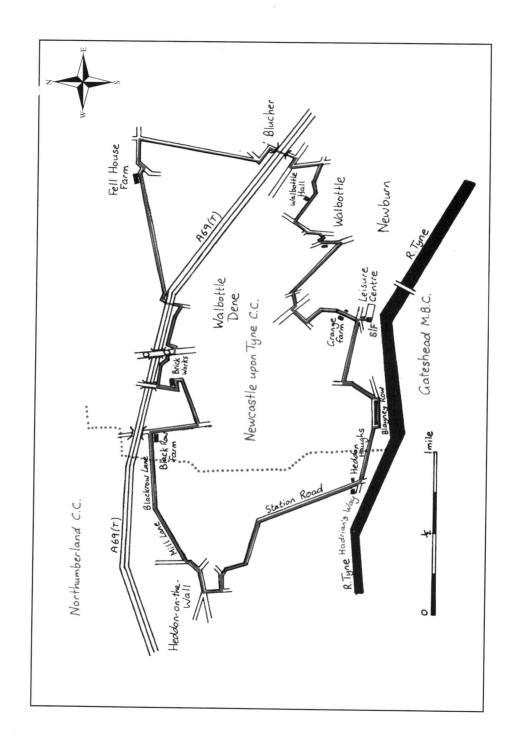

6. Humpty Dumpty...

Circuit of Newburn, Walbottle, Throckley and Heddon on the Wall

Distance:	**9.5 miles (15.3 Km.)**
Level:	**Medium**
Maps:	**Ordnance Survey Pathfinder 548 'Blaydon & Pruhoe'**
Facilities:	**Newburn Leisure Centre: toilets, changing, showers, vending machines for snacks and drinks. Toilets, drinks and pub grub available at Percy Arms (Throckley), Three Tuns and The Swan (Heddon).**
Parking:	**Newburn Leisure Centre or Tyne Riverside Park nearby.**

Introduction

A tour through the fields and lanes of the Tyne Valley to the west of Newcastle. It is easy to imagine how it must have looked before many of the new roads and houses were built. Even today it is amazing how quickly you leave the suburbs for open country.

This is a more difficult route with an uphill start. The effort is rewarded by an exciting 40+ mph downhill run from Heddon with panoramic views of the Tyne Valley. Most of the route is on good quality bridleways and quiet tarmac lanes.

One January Sunday after heavy rain I was out cycling with my friend Kevin. The muddy track at the top of Walbottle Dene had become a stream. At the top of the hill, judging by the classy machines on show, a mountain bike race had been run earlier. Expecting a friendly greeting from the participants we looked up, but they were all looking down at our bikes. I can only imagine their disappointment as they saw our second-hand heavyweights.

Route Description

Start opposite the end of the access road to the Leisure Centre car park. **(#1)** Go **SO** north up the steep tarmac bridleway past 'Grange Farm' (L). Continue through wood with dene (L). At top **TR** past rear terrace of cream coloured houses (L). At gate **TL** into housing estate then **TR** up hill to main road. **TR** at main road then **TL** up 'Briar Lane'. 'Walbottle Dene' will be facing you at the end of the street. Go through metal gate and **TR** onto bridleway through 'The Winning'. This track is on private land so please stick to the path which is a public right of way. **SO** to gate at end of track. **(#9) TL** immediately back on yourself and down stony hill on old road into dene. Go past sheds (L), take fork to **R** then **TR** on hairpin bend and go up steep hill round to **L**. At top of hill with terrace of stone houses opposite **TL** up main road. **TR** after public house 'The Percy Arms'. At the end of a short road you will see the stone gates to 'Walbottle Hall' (L).

Bear **R** of the gates onto the Public Byway signposted 'Blucher'. This is a very old road and the large cobblestones make progress difficult for the first 150 metres. Follow road **L** and **R** then **SO** uphill under power lines. At crossroads **TL** onto path. **SO** past playground (R) to main road and **TR**. Pass 'Blucher Social Club' (L) then **TL** at bus shelter to tunnel under A69(T). At the end of the tunnel go through barrier and **TL** onto wide tarmac path. Follow path to **R** then almost immediately **TL** over barrier and onto gravel track between bushes following power lines overhead. **SO** through a series of gates and past houses (R). At main road **(#9) TL** downhill for about 600 metres.

At bend to L **TR** into 'Fell House Farm' onto bridleway past farm (R). **SO** long straight then downhill to join tarmac road through tunnel under the A69(T). About 30 metres from the end of the underpass **(#9) TR** and go up muddy hill between bushes to rejoin tarmac road at the top. **SO** past storage depot (L), bear **L** to gate in chainlink fence.

TR up short hill and **TR** onto main road. At the first roundabout **TL** towards brickworks entrance then immediately **TR** up tarmac lane with the brickworks (L). At T junction with bridge over A69(T) (R) **TL** down stony road towards farm buildings.

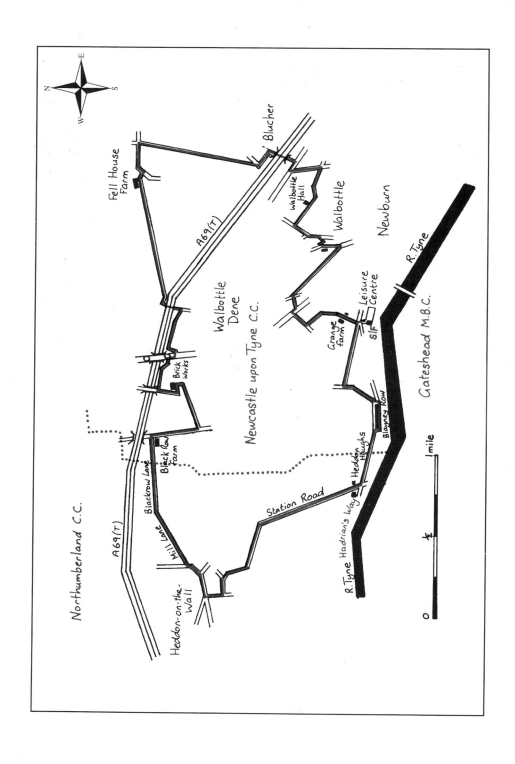

TL then **TR** through farm, past fence at back of factory (L) and onto bridleway. At T junction **TR** onto 'Drove Road'. 'Black Row Farm' ahead has a riding school and there may be horses on the road. Remember to show consideration for riders, slow down to pass, before resuming your journey. At the farm, just before the tunnel under the A69(T), **TL** onto 'Blackrow Lane'.

About halfway along this road's name changes to 'Mill Lane'. You should be able to see and hear the A69(T) (R). At end of lane **SO** up short hill to T junction and **TL** at main road. Pass sign for 'Heddon on the Wall' and bear **R** into village. **(#12 and #7)**

Past garage (L) **TL** into 'Towne Gate' and **TL** again, signposted 'Public Library' **(#12)** past 'The Swan' (R). At library (L) the road forks, **TR** downhill onto 'Station Road'. This is a very steep and exciting descent with several tight turns. Enjoy the ride and the view but watch out for oncoming cars and pedestrians. **SO** under power lines to farm buildings ahead.

SO through farm **(SO#1)** and **TL** before yellow gas main marker through gateway. **SO** to row of terraced cottages. **TR** then **TL** onto road to pass in front of the terrace. At the end of the houses **TL** then immediately **TR** onto bridleway and continue **SO** to cross footbridge. Immediately **TR** onto track through small wood. Follow narrow track to finish at 'Newburn Leisure Centre'. **(#1)**

City Slicker *Publications*

This is the first in a series of guides covering a variety of locations in the Tyne and Wear area. Other 'City Slicker' initiatives will include guided rides run in conjunction with various local councils and the publication of 'City Slicker' routes in magazines, newspapers and leaflets.

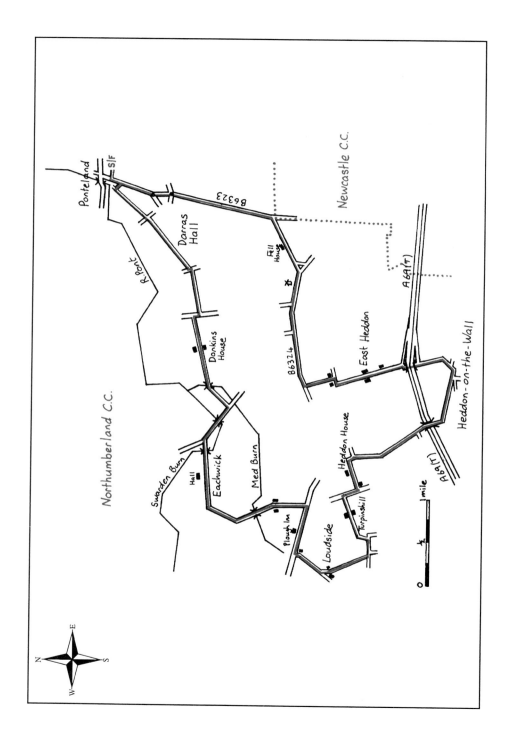

7. The Mekon
Circuit from Ponteland via Eachwick and Heddon

Distance: 15.5 miles (24.9 Km.)

Level: Medium

Maps: Ordnance Survey Pathfinder 535 'Ponteland'; 548 'Blaydon & Prudhoe'

Facilities: Changing, showers, toilets and refreshments at Ponteland Sports Centre. Cafes in Ponteland and Darras Hall. Toilets, drinks and pub grub at the 'Plough Inn' (Stamfordham Road) and 'Three Tuns' (Heddon).

Parking: Ponteland Sports Centre, Callerton Lane, Ponteland on A696(T) north west of Newcastle.

Introduction

This route is a good example of what looks straightforward on a map not matching what you actually find on the ground. In summer it is a moderate run; but attempted, as I first did, during the wettest January this century it was very heavy going in places.

Some of the bridleways over fields between Darras Hall and Heddon are difficult to find. Thankfully the blue arrows are still evident on most of the gates to guide your way.

You have a legal right to use these bridleways and new laws introduced recently make the duties and responsibilities of cyclists and farmers clear. Bridleways at the edges of fields must not be disturbed. Those across fields, although they can be worked by farmers, must be 'made convenient for use' usually within 24 hours. If you find a place where you think that the law is being broken report the problem to the rights of way department of the appropriate local authority. And remember, you are entitled to follow the route, even if it means riding over a crop.

Route Description

Leave the Sports Centre by the access road and **TL** at the main road. **SO** for 150 metres. Ignore the first footpath but **TR** through barrier onto second footpath signposted 'West Road 1/4'. **(TL Link#1)**. **SO** through second barrier, immediately **TL** and head towards tennis courts ahead. Just before these **TL** onto disused railway line and go **SO** between trees. **SO** over road to public bridleway opposite signposted 'The Broadway 3/ 4 Western Way 1'. At the end of the track go through gate onto red brick surface. Continue **SO** past church (L) to T junction with road. **TL** and immediately **TR** onto paved path between shops and garage. Behind shops bear **L** and then **SO** through gateway onto public bridleway signposted 'Western Way 1/2 Medburn 13/4'. **SO** to main road. Ignore the track ahead and **TR** then first **TL** onto 'The Crescent'. **SO** to end of the street and onto public bridleway signposted 'Dissington Bridge 1m.' Continue on this track with open fields either side and **SO** through farm. The bridleway goes downhill and over the 'Med Burn'. As the route goes uphill the good surface becomes a rutted field track with a hedge and old trees (R). At the end of the climb follow the track round to the **L** at the edge of the field and **SO** downhill to T junction with road. **TR** and go downhill, cross bridge over 'Swarden Burn' and continue uphill. Take next **TL** signposted 'Eachwick Wylam'.

SO downhill, over hump-back bridge and uphill into 'Eachwick'. 'Dissington Hall' will be visible in the distance (R). Pass 'Eachwick Hall' (R) and leave village on uphill road. Follow this road round to the **L** and then downhill through a series of easy bends. Eventually the road goes uphill between buildings and on to a T junction with the B6324. **TR** signposted 'Stamfordham 3 Matfen 7'.

Go **SO** past the 'Plough Inn' public house (R) and take the next **TL** at stone cottage signposted 'Loudside Leager House'. Bear to **R** past farm (L) then **SO** to fork in road at the next farm. **TL** signposted 'Public Bridleway Turpinshill 11/4'. Past barn (L) go through gate and **SO** across field. There is no obvious path but as you crest the hill, head for the gate in the fence opposite, by the big trees. There are two gates and a small bridge over a ditch.

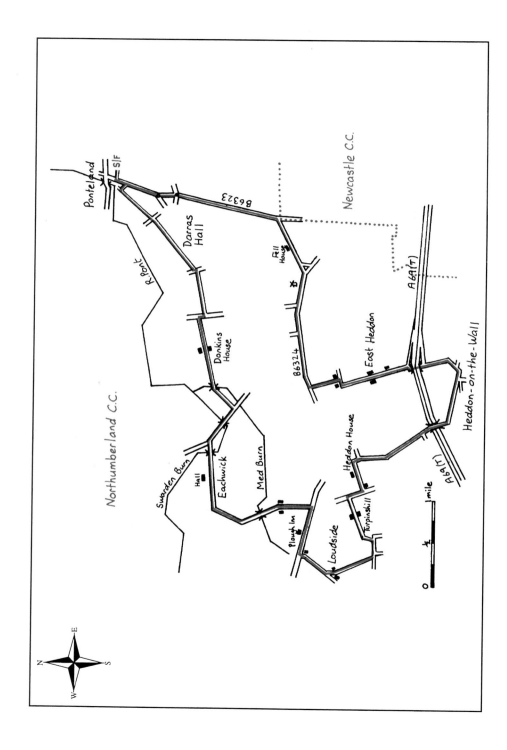

Beyond these **TR** through a third gate then **TL** and follow the narrow track at the field edge uphill with trees (L). At the top go through gate onto tarmac road. **TL** and go **SO** through gate and uphill on farm track ahead. Where the track bears R at metal barrier **TL** through gate and go down path for about 50 metres to metal gate. Though the gate **TR** into field and follow the edge of field uphill towards trees at 'Turpinshill' ahead. Again there is no obvious track but bear **R** near the farm buildings to the **R** of the two metal gates. Follow the road between the farm buildings and go **SO** downhill to T junction with road.

TR downhill for 400 metres then **TL** onto public bridleway signposted 'Heddon Steads 1/2'. Go **SO** past farm buildings (L) and follow road round to **R**. As the road bends L go **SO** deeply rutted farm track through gate and **SO** down field. At bottom of field go through small gate ahead onto narrow path following wall (L). Join tarmac road and continue **SO** down then uphill to join the B6318 and cross bridge over A69(T). **(#12)** down then round to **L** then uphill to Heddon.

Follow this road down and round to **L** then uphill to Heddon.

At 'Three Tuns' public house **TL** to join B6528. **(#6 and #12)** Continue round to **L** then downhill and under the A69(T). **TL** uphill on single track road signposted 'East Heddon'. **SO** uphill through farm buildings. Follow road round sharp bend to **R** and then **TL** at next junction with farm houses either side. **SO** downhill to T junction and **TR** onto B6324. Continue on this road past two turnings (L). About 400 metres after the disused windmill (L) the road forks with the main road going R. Take **L** fork onto single track road. Continue **SO** to T junction. **TL** onto main road. **SO** at first, then **TR** at second roundabouts following B6323 to 'Ponteland' past high school (R). **(TR Link#1) SO** then **TR** and **TR** back into sports centre and finish.

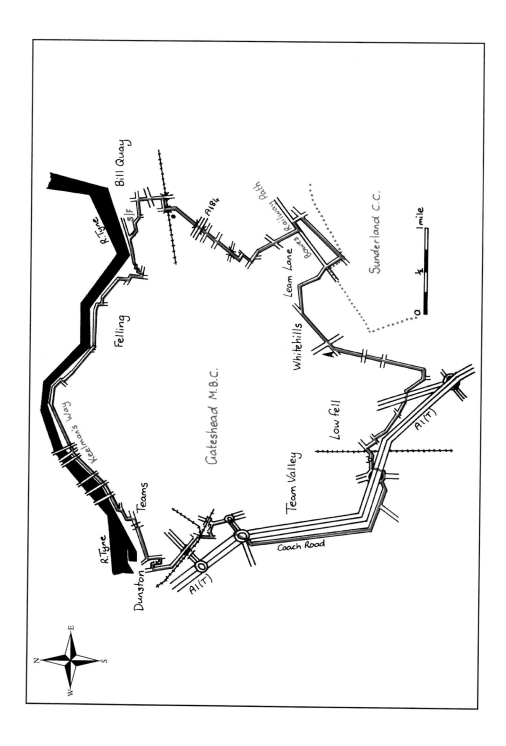

8. Walk Away Renee
Circuit from Bill Quay Farm via Whitehills and Team Valley

Distance:	**15.9 miles (25.5 Km.)**
Level:	**Medium**
Maps:	**Ordnance Survey Pathfinder 549 'Newcastle upon Tyne'; 562 'Washington'**
Facilities:	**Toilets and refreshments at Bill Quay Farm and Safeway supermarket on Team Valley half way round. Pubs and restaurants at the quayside.**
Parking:	**Bill Quay Community Farm, Pelaw, Gateshead.**

Introduction

For variety of scenery this is one of the best routes in this guide. Along the Bowes Railway Path you are in the middle of open country with a panorama of the coast from South Shields to Blyth as a backdrop. Further on there are good views south down the Team Valley into County Durham. Probably most spectacular of all is the sweep of the River Tyne seen from Bill Quay Farm right at the end of the ride.

However this is also a trip of stark contrasts. It passes through inner city housing estates, old industrial land and derelict factories as well as recently built commercial areas, modern housing and newly developed parkland.

At the end of the Team Valley the path follows the route of the road train which transported millions of visitors round the 'National Garden Festival' held at Gateshead in 1990. Although much of the land has been developed for housing the original landscaping has been left for public use at 'Eslington Park'. The only area still closed is the riverside park alongside the spectacular Dunston Staithes. Hopefully this will be accessible to the public in the near future.

Route Description

Leave 'Bill Quay Farm' (**#3**) by the main entrance and **TL** into 'Hainingwood Terrace'. **TR** at crossroads onto 'Station Road' and go **SO** to end. Cross main road and **SO** past over waste ground towards footbridge ahead. Just before bridge **TR** downhill on path running parallel with Metro Line (L). At 'Pelaw Station' **TL** over footbridge. **SO** from end of bridge for about 50 metres. Just before road **TR** onto disused mineral line. Go **SO** under bridge, across road, past school (R), across next road and continue uphill. After about 150 metres the path forks. Take the **R** fork and **SO** uphill over road bridge and past 'Colgate Junior School' (R).

From the end of the track go **SO** paved path with bungalow (R). At end **TL, TR & TL** round brick building into estate road 'Creslow'. At the T junction with garages opposite **TR** up short steep hill and **TL** at T junction. Ahead is 'Eastview Terrace' (R). Bear to **L** then **SO** onto narrow bridleway past allotments (R) and uphill to fork in path with paved section and electricity sub-station ahead to R. Take **L** fork across grass onto tarmac pathway. **SO** across road using ramps and **SO** to main road at end. **TL** downhill for 150 metres then **TR** onto 'Public Bridle Path'. After 50 metres **TR** onto disused railway line. **SO** uphill to metal bridge over culvert just before power lines cross above the track. (**SO Link#3**) **TR** down the very steep embankment past sheds (R) and go uphill on bridle path to main road. Cross road and **SO** on narrow path with school (R). Keep metal fence and houses **L** and follow the path round to open ground and T junction with track. **TL** and continue round with houses (L). **SO** towards two radio masts ahead and cross over disused railway line. Just before houses ahead **TL** onto black gravel cycle track. **SO** long straight track with another radio mast ahead.

Cross the main road to road opposite then **TL** onto Public Bridle Path, radio mast (R). **SO** downhill, golf course (R), under bridge, through various sets of barriers and **SO** at junction of paths. (**#10**) Finally path bears to **R**, ignore fork to L, and continue **SO** towards flats ahead. Just before flats **TL** into tunnel under main road. **SO** downhill and cross road to path signposted 'Team Colliery Railway'.

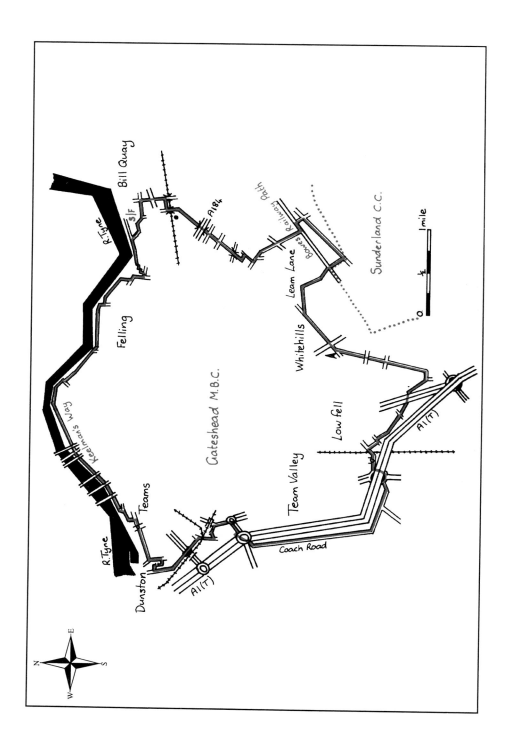

SO narrow steep descent and bear **R** at bottom. Go between houses onto road and **TL** onto 'Salcombe Gardens'. Bear **R** to T junction with main road. **SO** at first roundabout, supermarket (R), to roundabout under A1(T). Take third exit signposted 'Lady Park', past houses (R) to L bend in road. Go **SO** onto 'Coach Road' and continue with A1(T) (R). **(#10)** Finally this road becomes a street with houses (L). **SO** to end and onto paved path to subway. Go down into subway, keep to **R** and cross A1(T). At end of bridge **TL** into another subway and follow path to T junction with road. **TR** to main road then **TL** and follow road round. Take the 'Gateshead B1426' exit at the roundabout.

Just before railway bridge **TL** then **TL** again through barrier onto red tarmac path. At next bridge (L) **TR** under bridge into 'Eslington Park'. Cross 'River Teams' bearing **L** at fork, uphill past pyramidical shaped mounds (R). **SO** towards yellow triangular bridge support. **SO** under this and over bridge. Keep to this path past flats (L) and new houses (R). After short uphill to 'Swan Court' old persons home **TR** through barrier and onto estate. Follow road to **R** then **SO** to second **TL** to T junction with main road.

TL onto main road then first **TR** signposted 'Gateshead Newcastle'. **(#2)** **SO** past gasworks (R) to roundabout. **SO** to 'Rose Street' then immediately **TL** before the houses onto stony path. Follow path to **R** then fork to **L** and go downhill, under bridges onto road past oil depot (L). **SO** up short hill to junction. **(#2 and #3)** **TR** and **TL** signposted 'Gateshead East Industrial Estate'. **SO** under 'Tyne Bridge', past 'Baltic Flour Mill' (L) and ready mixed cement works (L). At end **TR** up short hill then first **TL**, **SO** to end of road and onto riverside path. **SO** downhill and take path ahead along the riverbank. **TL** and **TR** at hairpin bend and continue alongside river. At 'Riverside Lodge' hotel **TR** up steep hill and go **SO** through car park.

At junction before factory unit (L) **TL** on uphill path between trees. Follow this path round to T junction with road. **TL** and follow road to **R** past main entrance of Courtaulds Coatings (L). Take first **TL** onto 'Abbotsford Road'. Just before first industrial unit (L) **TL** onto path, follow path round behind unit and downhill at back of paint works (L). At bottom of the hill go **SO** the path until it leaves the riverside and enters a small copse. **(#3) TR** uphill onto a steep gravelly path bearing to **L** at the top and **SO** to finish at 'Bill Quay Farm'.

 ### Cycling in South Tyneside

South Tyneside Council is developing a Borough wide, linked network of cycle routes. These will enable and encourage more people to participate in the recreational, health and environmental benefits of cycling. The area has much to offer, with a relatively flat topography, a beautiful coastline and spectacular riverside views.

A Coastal Cycleway is due to open in 1995 linking the Foreshore and Souter Lighthouse. In addition to the already established routes (see page 59) two other major projects are planned. The first will extend the Bowes Railway Path through Monkton Cycleway to link with the Gateshead and on, to form part of the Cumbria to Tyneside Cycle Route, C2C. Secondly, with the redevelopment of a former colliery site, the Westoe Cycleway will be established over the next few years. This will link the Foreshore with South Shields town centre and the Shields Ferry. In addition, the River Don Route is to be upgraded for cyclists in the near future.

As part of the Council's policy to improve road safety and reduce road traffic accidents, cycling facilities are being improved. The Road Safety Section provides Cycle Proficiency Training in all the Borough's primary schools.

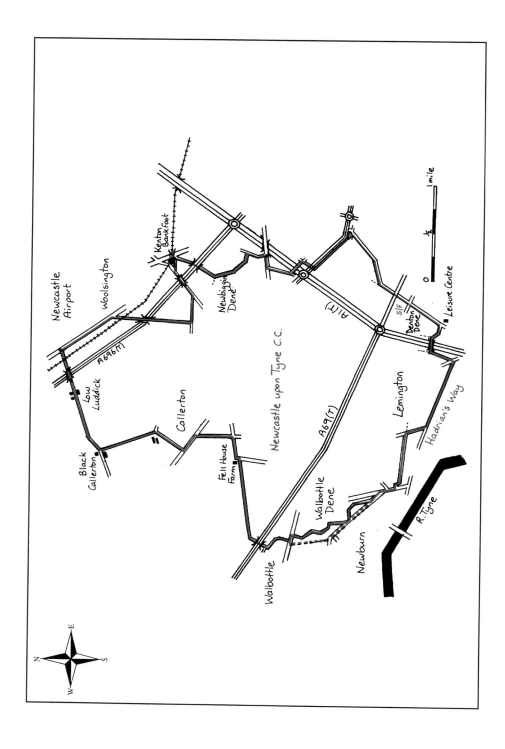

9. Double Dare
Denton, Newbiggin and Walbottle Denes

Distance: 13.3 miles (21.4 Km.)

Level: Medium/Hard

Maps: Ordnance Survey Pathfinder 548 'Blaydon & Prudhoe'; 549 'Newcastle upon Tyne'

Facilities: Toilets, pubs and shops close to start. Toilets and snacks at Cowell's Garden Centre, Woolsington, halfway round. Various pubs on route. Toilets and vending machines at Scotswood Sports Centre.

Parking: Denton Burn Library, West Road, Newcastle, 3 miles west of the city centre on the A186 (A69T).

Introduction

As a child in the late 1950s and early 1960s I used to play with friends in Denton Dene. It was a lot wilder and deeper then. I remember it being filled with bluebells in the spring. We used to 'dare' each other to accomplish dangerous challenges on the steep rocky sides. A 'double dare' meant that you had to go first! It would make a good motto for off road cyclists.

Walbottle Dene has been spared landscaping and is much more like the Denton Dene of my memories. It is also where I sustained my first off road cycling injury when, much to the amusement of my 'friends' John and Kevin, my front wheel slipped and I fell head first into the stream while crossing one of the stony fords. Despite the laughs the resulting gash in my leg was quite serious.

Apart from Walbottle Dene, for which I have suggested a less strenuous alternative path, this is a reasonably easy route with moderate gradients throughout. The steepest section is the short climb out of Denton Dene right at the end of the ride.

Route Description

Leave the car park, cross the main road (A186) and go SO path up wide grassed area opposite. Follow path diagonally to R across field then SO past football pitches (L) towards bus depot ahead. Pass depot (L), cross road and bear L onto cycle track. At dual carriageway TL onto cycle track running alongside road. SO at first roundabout. Just before next roundabout TR to cross both carriageways and go SO path past undulating field (R). TL into 'Chessar Avenue', then TL and cross footbridge over A1(T). At end of bridge TR and cross field towards flats with green roofs ahead. The path disappears in the middle, so use the obvious grass track instead. At the far side of the field pick up the path again past flats (L) to the road. TR and SO to roundabout. TL into 'Etal Way' and follow road round to R. At the shops (R) TL down path with allotments (L). Go through barrier, ignore stony path ahead and TL onto tarmac path, up short rise SO crossroads of paths then follow path down to R into centre of 'Newbiggin Dene'.

SO along path taking fork L to tunnel. SO through tunnel and uphill. Follow track ahead, under barrier and round to R. At main road TL back on yourself, up paved path with Metro Line (R). SO through station car park and past 'Bank Foot' station (R). TL at main road and then SO across roundabouts and bridge over A696(T). After 100 metres TR onto lane, before house with wooden fence. Follow lane to L then SO through metal gate onto tarmac pathway between bushes. After 400 metres TR through metal gates onto bridleway. SO to bridge over A696(T) and Metro crossing. Dismount and push your bike over the track. SO to the main road, TL then SO to roundabout.

Before 'Wheatsheaf' public house TL onto road signposted 'Black Callerton 11/4'. Cross Metro track, roundabouts, A696(T) and SO past 'Low Luddick': (TR Link#1) Continue on road to first TL at 'East Cottage' (R). Go down single track road past terraces of houses (R). Bear R ignoring road to L and go SO past 'The Burnside' public house (R). At T junction TL and go uphill for 200 metres. TR onto Public Bridleway signposted 'North Walbottle 1/3'. SO to main road and TR downhill. After 600 metres TR into 'Fell House Farm' onto bridleway past farm (R).

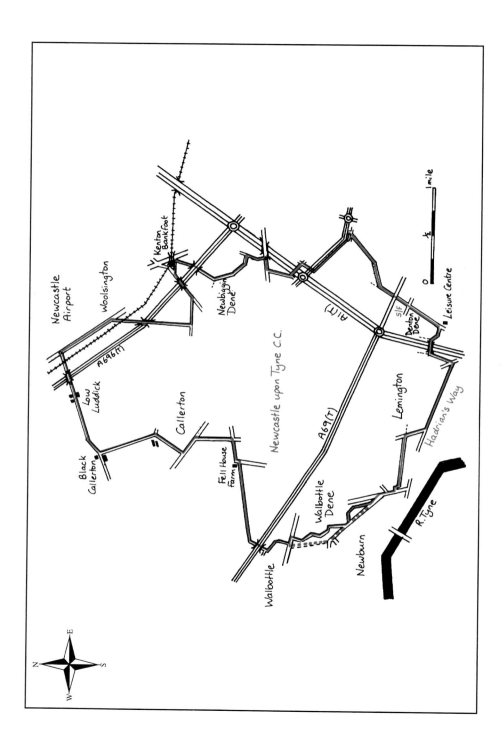

SO long straight then downhill to join tarmac road through tunnel under A69(T). **(TR#6)** Go **SO** then bear **L** into trees following the undulating path round into 'Walbottle Dene'. Keep the stream to your **R**, finish uphill to road.

* If you want the easy way down then cross the main road **TR** then **TL** up the stone steps onto the path. This is a footpath so push for the first 400 metres to the narrow gate at road. **TL** through this gate then **TL** through the next gateway onto the bridlepath. **SO** over barrier to end of path. At this point you rejoin the main route.

* For the 'Double Dare' cross the road **TL** then **TR** down stepped path into dene. Continue on undulating path, keep to the **L** after the narrow bridge and follow the main path which crosses a series of steep fords. Eventually the path climbs steeply. **TL** onto bridleway for 100 metres then **TL** on steep path with steps back down into the dene. **SO** past sheds (R) onto road and **SO** up the stony hill. **(#6)**

Go **SO** past council depot (L) to main road. **TR** downhill past derelict factories (R), waste reception site (L) and road, 'Weight Limit 2 Tons' (L). Take next **TL** on short road which curves round to **R** through barrier to metal gate. Join bridleway to **R** of gate. Bear to the **L** and then **SO** uphill under two sets of power lines. At junction of paths **TR** downhill on tarmac path, through gate and **SO** to join cycleway. **(#2)** Follow the cycleway until it joins road. Cross the road at crossing and **SO** uphill on path with A1(T) (R). **TR** across footbridge **(#2)** and go **SO** path towards Scotswood Sports and Leisure Centre. **TL** and go downhill into 'Denton Dene' which is now a nature reserve. Keep bearing **R** and go **SO** up centre of dene. At top of dene go up steep hill, **TR** halfway up hill. **SO** across road and onto path up wide grassed area. **SO** to car park by library and finish.

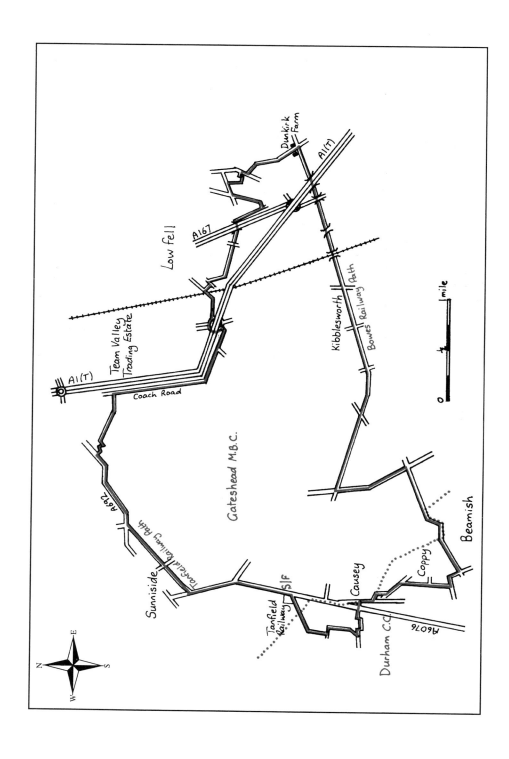

10. Derailed or Derailleur

Circuit from Tanfield Railway to Beamish and Bowes Museums

Distance:	15.5 miles (24.9 Km.)
Level:	Hard
Maps:	Ordnance Survey Pathfinder 562' Washington'; 549 'Newcastle upon Tyne'
Facilities:	Toilets, drinks and snacks at Safeways supermarket halfway round. Various pubs on route.
Parking:	Tanfield Railway Museum. Take A692 'Consett' road from A1(T) near Gateshead. Follow signs for 'Tanfield Railway' from Sunniside.

Introduction

For ten years the organisation 'Sustrans' has been building new routes for cyclists, walkers and disabled people throughout Britain. Their dream is to develop a network of thousands of miles of traffic free routes across the UK. It is a vision I am happy both to share and support.

Part of this tour is on the Bowes Railway Path which is being developed by Gateshead Council to link the South Tyneside Cycleway, the Tanfield Railway Path and the Sustrans 'C2C' route from Whitehaven and Workington to Tyneside.

Enthusiasts for steam railways and industrial archaeology will love this tour as it visits three of the region's best working museums: The Bowes Railway, the world's only preserved standard gauge rope hauled railway (1826); Beamish Museum, a reconstruction of life in the north east in 1913; and Tanfield Railway, the oldest railway in the world (1725) with Causey Arch the first railway bridge ever built (1727).

This is probably the most varied route in the book and includes disused railway lines, bridleways, country lanes and a couple of road sections.

Route Description

Leave 'Tanfield Railway' car park and **TL** onto A6076. **SO** uphill for a magnificent view of Tyneside from the top. At junction (R) bear **L** downhill and then round to **R**. Just before the first houses (R) **TR** through barriers onto Public Bridleway (#11) and go **SO** between trees. Continue **SO** through barriers and across road onto Bridle Path opposite. Follow the path downhill and through barriers to main road (A692). (#11) **TR** and follow road downhill through woods in a series of bends. Eventually the road turns uphill with stone wall (R). Just before first houses (R) **TR** and go through stepped gap in the wall onto track signposted 'Public Bridleway Coach Road 2/3'. Follow the track through trees downhill, round to **L** and join gravelly path. This path zig-zags round a series of grassy mounds before bearing **R** to pass children's playground and playing fields (R). Pass changing rooms (L) and go **SO** down steep red tarmac road to T junction. (#8)

TR onto 'Coach Road' and follow this undulating road with A1(T) and 'Team Valley Trading Estate' (L). Continue **SO** to T junction then **TL** and follow this road round to roundabout under the A1(T). **TL** at the second exit signposted 'Low Fell' and go **SO** past supermarket (L), across second roundabout and over railway line on bridge. Take next **TR** onto 'Salcombe Gardens'. At the end of the street bear **L** uphill then just before number 59 **TR** towards open ground. Follow path ahead signposted 'Public Bridleway Allerdene Park' round to **R** and uphill between bushes. Cross road and continue on path opposite signposted 'Durham Road 325 metres'. **SO** uphill, through underpass and **TR** to follow path across level area, **L** downhill, **L** uphill finally bearing **R** to barrier and crossroads of paths. (#8)

TR onto stony lane and take next **TR** onto 'Western View' with bungalows (L). At end of street **TL** and **TL** round 'Haigh Terrace'. **TR** up 'Armitage Gardens' to T junction with main road. **TR** then immediately **TL** signposted 'Public Bridleway Dunkirk Farm'. **SO** to crossroads just through farm (**TL Link#3** and 'Bowes Railway Museum'). **TR** downhill on disused railway track.

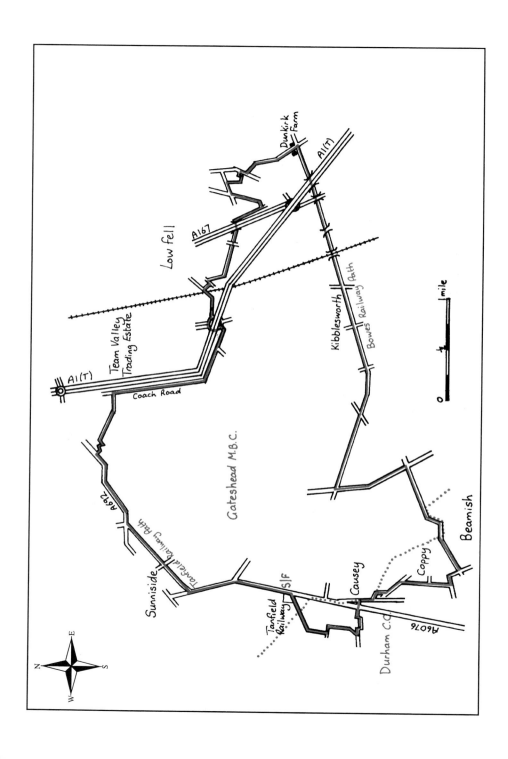

Continue **SO** under a series of bridges and over 'River Team' to road. Cross road to Public Bridle Path opposite. Continue **SO** to outskirts of 'Kibblesworth' where track forks. Go **SO** uphill on muddy track with houses (R) to crossroads with rough tarmac road where you will see the first of a series of wood and sandstone sculptures (R). Go **SO** gravel track which bears **R** to main road. Cross road and take track opposite by sculpture 'Bowes Railway Path'. This disused railway track goes steadily uphill between bushes. Continue **SO** until path bears **L** up steep ramp to road ahead. Go through barrier and **TL** onto road. **SO** down this road for just under 1 mile to Public Bridleway (R) signposted 'Beamish Hall 11/2'. **TR** and follow the main track downhill through a series of bends. Eventually the path levels out and follows 'Beamish Burn' (L) towards 'Beamish Hall' ahead. At T junction in front of gates to hall **TR** (TL for 'Beamish Museum') and follow road up and round to **L**.

Take next **TR** uphill. 'Coppy Lane' is a permissive path, there is no public right of way for cyclists. Please keep to the track and respect the privacy of those living along the lane. Please keep your speed down and take extra care past the riding school. Go **SO** uphill until the road bends to R. At this point go **SO** through gate and continue uphill. At fork in track bear round to L and go **SO** until the track bends to L at farm entrance. Leave track here **SO** on narrow path through trees. The ground is very cut up and you may have to push. Follow track through wood to join paved road downhill to T junction. **TR** onto road with 'Beamish Park Hotel' (R) and 'Causey Arch Inn' ahead.

TL downhill before public house, cross A6076(T) and go **SO** over railway crossing. This road bends steeply downhill. At the bottom of the hill **TR** downhill through metal gate. This area is liable to flooding. Avoiding the water take the track ahead which follows edge of field and fence (R). The track' goes uphill then round to **L** towards ruined farm ahead. Before farm **TR** through gate and **SO** track between fields. Bear to **R** at end of field and uphill to gate. Through gate continue **SO** with 'Tanfield Railway' (L). Cross bridge over railway and **TL** into car park and finish.

GATESHEAD
METROPOLITAN BOROUGH COUNCIL

Cycling in Gateshead

There is a growing number of off road cycle ways in the Borough of Gateshead. These are currently being supplemented by a number of shared on road/footpath routes. This network gives access to some of the most varied and beautiful scenery in Tyneside. Gateshead's main routes are:

The Keelman's Way - an on and off road route following the south bank of the River Tyne from Wylam to Bill Quay, a distance of 13.7 miles.
The Derwent Walk Country Park - one of the largest country parks in the north east. A scenic 12.5 mile off road cycle route starts at the Swalwell Visitor Centre where you can obtain further information about the park.
Blaydon Burn - A 1.5 mile off road route up this beautiful wooded valley to the hamlet of Blaydon Burn.
Tanfield Railway Path - running from Lobley Hill to Sunniside, this route will be further enhanced when improvements at Watergate Colliery are completed.

A major reclamation scheme is currently under way on the Bowes Railway Path to create an off road route which will connect with the Monkton Mineral Line and the Tanfield Railway Path.
Other initiatives to promote cycling include the 'Marking the Way Project' which is placing sculptures along many of Gateshead's routes. A 'Countryside Events' Programme includes several guided cycle tours in and around Gateshead.
You can find routes in Gateshead on pages 11, 15, 19, 39, 47, 51 & 59.
For further information, an events programme and two free leaflets 'Derwent Walk Country Park' and 'The Keelman's Way' contact:
The Countryside Team, Gateshead MBC, Civic Centre, Gateshead, NE8 1HH.
Telephone (0191) 477 1011

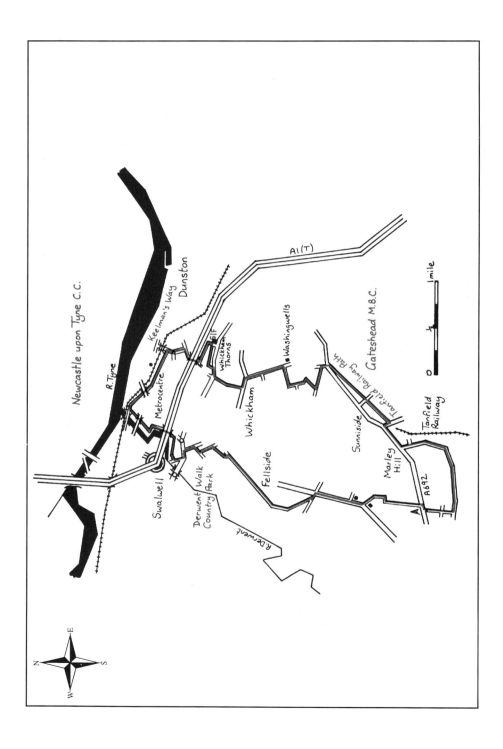

Newcastle upon Tyne C.C.

R. Tyne

Keelman's Way

Dunston

A1(T)

Whickham Thorns

Washingwells

Whickham

Metrocentre

Swalwell

Derwent Walk Country Park

Fellside

R. Derwent

Gateshead M.B.C.

Tanfield Railway Path

Sunniside

Marley Hill

A692

Tanfield Railway

A

N
W   E
S

0   1 mile

11. Tracks of My Tears

'A Ride in the Great North Forest' from Whickham Thorns via Sunniside, Marley Hill and Swalwell

Distance:	**11.6 miles (18.7 Km.)**
Level:	**Hard**
Maps:	**Ordnance Survey Pathfinder 548 'Blaydon & Prudhoe'; 549 'Newcastle upon Tyne'; '561 Consett & Rowlands Gill'; '562 Washington'**
Facilities:	**Toilets, changing and vending machines at Whickham Thorns. Several pubs on route. Shops in Sunniside and Blaydon.**
Parking:	**Whickham Thorns Centre, Market Lane, Gateshead. Take turning for 'Whickham/Dunston' off the A1(T) road south of Gateshead and follow signs for Centre.**

Introduction

This was the last route to be completed for the guide. I first rode it the other way round. When I finished I decided that it might be better done clockwise. When I finally got down to recording it properly I was pleased to find that my hunch had been right. When ridden as I describe it below it gives magnificent views, especially between Tanfield and Blaydon. The drawback of doing it this way is the very steep start followed by the uphill haul from 'Washingwell Woods' to 'Blackamoor Hill'. You can, of course ride this, and any of the other routes in this book any way round you like. I hope you will.

Much of this ride is in the Great North Forest, a major new initiative to create well wooded countryside providing a range of accessible recreational facilities for local people. This must be a 'City Slicker's' dream come true!

Route Description

Leave the car park and go uphill on the path through the Centre grounds past the assault course and picnic area. At the top **TL** and go through the gate to the main road. **TR** on road until just past 'Crowley Hotel' (R) then **TL** uphill onto 'Duckpool Lane'. Go **SO** steeply uphill. Where estate road joins from R continue uphill, past 'St Mary's RC Primary School' (R). Finally the lane levels out and meets the 'Whickham Highway' at T junction. **TL**, go past police station (L) then immediately **TR** onto path between houses signposted 'Watergate 1'.

Go **SO** uphill through houses and out into open fields on bumpy track. Continue to turning just before buildings at 'Washingwells' (L). **TR** downhill on bridlepath signposted 'Broom Lane 1/3'. Go **SO** past 'Washingwell Woods' (L) and follow track to **L** at end of field. Where the main path bears to R go **SO** down field edge to woods ahead. **SO** through gate, steeply downhill to stream and **TR** over footbridge. Ahead there is a very steep track uphill through the trees which follows a fence (L). Unless you are superhuman you will have to push up this to the T junction with a path at the top. **TL** and follow the path round keeping **R** at fork. At T junction **TR** up short lane to busy main road. **(#10)**

Cross the road and go **SO** up the public bridlepath opposite. Continue on this track uphill for some distance to barrier. Go through this, cross road and continue **SO** path opposite. Finally the path levels out a little and finishes at T junction with road. **(#10) TR** downhill to T junction with 'A692' and **TL** towards 'Consett'. Continue **SO** this road until it goes uphill into 'Marley Hill'. At 'St Cuthbert's Parish Church' (L) **TL** onto 'St Cuthbert's Road' signposted 'Public Bridleway Tanfield Railway'. Go **SO** with the church and graveyard (R) past turning (L) to the end of the street, through gate and uphill bearing to **R** on lane. At the top the way is a little unclear as there are several tracks across the derelict land. The main path bears **R** and goes downhill towards a small brick railway building ahead. **SO** past this building (R) and follow the bumpy track round **R**. At the fork in track **TR** uphill past house (R). At junction of tracks continue **SO** uphill towards radio mast and T junction with main road at top.

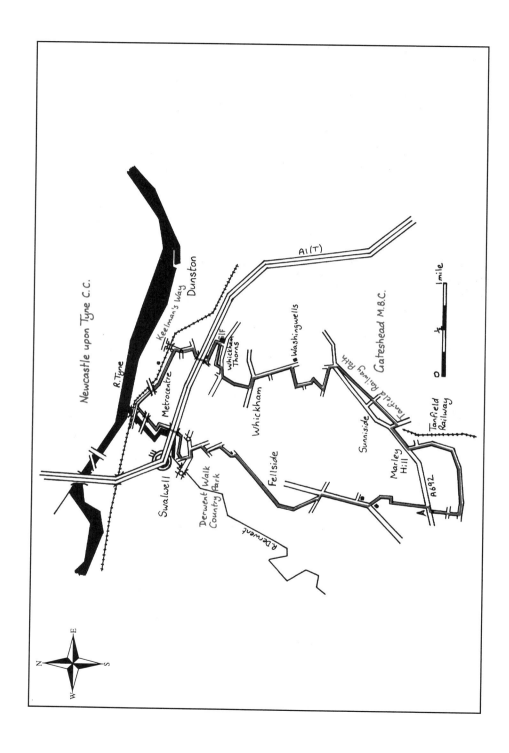

This is a dangerous crossing so **TR** and walk down the verge for 50 metres before crossing to bridlepath opposite. The sign reads 'Bridlepath Fellside 2/3' although there is no evidence on the ground of a right of way. Cross the stile and, remembering your rights, cycle down the edge of the field close to the fence (L). At the very bottom of this field **TR** for 20 metres, **TL** over stile and continue along the field edge with fence (R). Go through the gate ahead and **TL** onto the track which goes past the farm buildings (L) to T junction with road ahead.

TR and continue **SO** main road past 'Woodman's Arms' (R) and downhill past 'Whickham Golf Course' (L). Just past the golf club entrance (L) **TL** onto road downhill 'Unsuitable for Motors'. After 50 metres **TR** onto wide track. **SO** this undulating track which follows the valley side round, past turning for the 'Derwent Walk' (L) onto narrower path with housing estate (R). Where the track goes up **R** to road **TL** across the grassy slope to join a narrow path which goes steeply downhill between bushes. **TL** down steep estate road 'Woodhouse Lane'. Continue downhill and **SO** at end onto bridleway. Bear **R** past farm (L) to join track from L and go **SO** to T junction with main road.

TL downhill past 'The Poacher' and 'Borgognes' public houses (R) to traffic lights. **TL** onto main road. At 'Blaydon Rugby Club' (L) **TR** across road to join the 'South Tyne Cycleway' signposted 'Dunston 3 Swingbridge 5'. Just after 'Swalwell Cricket Club' (R) **TR** onto path signposted 'The Hurrocks 1/2'. Follow path under a bridge then **L** to a suspension type footbridge. **TR** before this and keep following the river (L), under the A1(T) and onto a riverside path with railings (L). Finally go under road bridge and where the 'Derwent' joins the 'River Tyne' **TR** onto the 'Keelman's Way'. **(#2)** Follow twisty path with the railway line (L) under road, past station (L) and 'Metrocentre' (R).

At main road **(#2) TR** and continue **SO** over roundabout towards 'Federation Brewery' ahead. Just before brewery **TR**, go through barrier and **SO** to T junction. **TL** and go under A1(T). Through the subway **TL** onto track with dual carriageway (L). Follow the track and **TR** uphill on stony path to 'Whickham Thorns' car park and finish.

Community Forests are large areas on the edge of towns and cities where environmental improvements will create well wooded countryside, offering a wide range of benefits to local people. Their guiding principles are to diversify the countryside for conservation, forestry, environmentally friendly agriculture, sport, recreation and the arts. Their aim is to develop multipurpose forests which will create better environments for people to cherish, use and enjoy.

The Great North Forest Plan, launched in 1994, is a major new initiative in the planning and development of South Tyneside's urban fringe. It is being carried forward through partnerships between local authorities, the Countryside Commission and The Forestry Commission.

The plan is to create a number of major 'gateway' recreation sites, linked by a network of multiuser routes for walking, cycling and horse riding. Smaller, more local gateways will offer access to long distance routes and key sites close to the urban edge. This will improve the quality of life in the area. It will help to achieve more community participation by providing facilities close to where people live. Because these are close to many urban areas it is not always necessary to use a car.

Several routes in this guide cross parts of the Great North Forest (see pages 39, 47, 51 & 59) If you want further information including a series of free cycling guides 'Rides in the Great North Forest' and a very useful leaflet 'Sport and Recreation' contact:

Sport and Recreation Officer, Great North Forest, The Grove, Birtley Lane, Birtley, Co.Durham, DH3 1AZ. Telephone (0191) 410 9066

12. ...Had a Great Fall
Additional Loop for Routes 6 & 7

Distance: 2.4 miles (3.9 Km.) or 3.2 miles (5.1 Km.) via Heddon Low Farm

Level: Very Hard

Maps: Ordnance Survey Pathfinder 548 'Blaydon & Prudhoe'

Facilities: Toilets, drinks and pub grub available at Three Tuns and The Swan in Heddon.

Parking: Plenty of parking in Heddon.

Introduction
This loop turns two outings into more challenging rides for the fit and adventurous, especially if you complete the full loop via Heddon Low Farm.

I first rode it one autumn Sunday morning. With wet and very muddy wheels from the ploughed field at Heddon Mill I flew off the end of the bridleway at Hill Head straight onto the steep and difficult descent with inevitable results. The ride up from Heddon Low Farm is very hard, I have not yet managed it without stopping for breath half way up.

Route Description
At Heddon (**#6 and #7**) just before the 'Three Tuns' Public House **TR** onto bridleway signposted 'A69 1/4'. **SO** through gate past 'Bays Leap Farm' (R) and down stony descent to paved road under A69(T). Through tunnel bear **R** then **TL** back on yourself through a small gate and up grassy path. **TR** and follow path at bottom of A69(T) embankment. The going on this path is very difficult, long grass and cut up by horses. You may be forgiven for pushing to halfway when it gets a little easier.

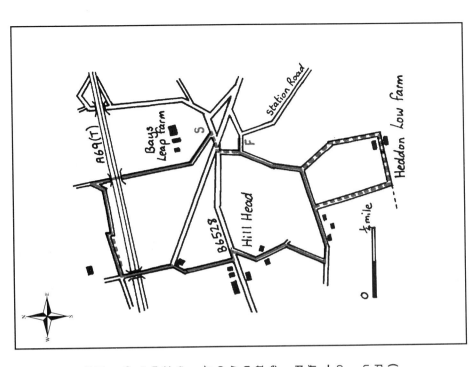

SO to small copse. ***TR** down the hill to an old stone wall. Go through an old gate and **TL** under power lines along the edge of the field keeping the dry stone wall **L**. At this point the bridleway disappears and, if the field is ploughed, progress is practically impossible.

*A nifty shortcut is to go **SO** into the copse through the gate. You will make out a narrow track between the trees close to the fence (L). It is obviously used by horses judging by the evidence left behind. At the end of the copse, rejoin the path.

SO through gate **TR** up short path to road. **(#7) TL** over A69(T) and go downhill on main road. At the bend to **L**, **TR** through metal 5 bar gate. Follow bridleway to **R** of house and garage. Bear **L** and then **SO** to main road. Through gate **TL** onto road then **TR** up steep hill signposted 'West Acres 1/2 Heddon Low Farm 1'. At the top there is a good view of the Tyne Valley (R).

SO to houses at 'Hill Head'. Go past the large white house (R) and bear to **L** of the car parking space and stone pillar with mushroom on the top down grassy lane into trees. This is a steep and bumpy descent, follow the obvious path through trees, bearing **R** halfway down, to lane at bottom of the wood. **TL** and **SO** bumpy lane past stone cottages (R). Look out for a magnificent view of the Tyne Valley and the outskirts of Tyneside (R).

At this point you may wish to **TR** downhill on the bridleway signposted 'Heddon Low Farm 1/2'. There is no obvious path so follow the edge of the field as closely as possible with hedge to **L**. At bottom of field **TL** signposted 'Public Bridleway'. **SO** past cowsheds, then **TL** up very steep gravelly hill back to the main road.

The alternative is to continue **SO** the road and up to the **L** past 'Heddon Banks Farm' (L). The road is still very steep and if you have pedalled right up from the bottom you will be feeling it by now. At the top **(SO #7) TR** signposted 'Public Library' to join 'Humpty Dumpty'. **(#6)**

Link Route 1. Duck
Callerton to Ponteland

Distance:	2.2 miles (3.5 Km.)
Level:	Easy
Maps:	Ordnance Survey Pathfinder 535 'Ponteland'.
Facilities:	None on Route

Introduction

This route links Route 9 'Double Dare' (page 43) with Route 7 'The Mekon' (page 35). It also joins Link Route 2 'Double Duck'.

This is a fairly new route, partly on the disused Newcastle to Ponteland railway line. There is still work being done on the middle part of the route by the disused mine. It passes between the landing lights of Newcastle Airport and if you catch a big aircraft taking off or landing I can promise a memorable experience.

Route Description

The route starts at 'Low Luddick' (**#9**) on the bridleway which goes north between the barn and the stone farmhouse. Go **SO** through gate, uphill and **TL** then **TR** past ruined stone building (L) to second gate. After gate **TL**, follow track through next gate and **TR** onto track past landing lights with view of runway (R). Continue **SO** downhill with view of 'Simonside Hills' ahead. At bottom of hill **TR** onto gravel track past ponds (L). Bear round to **L** at top of ponds and uphill to gate.

SO to tarmac road and bear **L** through gate onto wide lane and **SO** through gates to crossroads with tarmac road. Continue **SO** onto track which bears to **R**. At fork **TL** onto long straight path between bushes. **SO** to gate and main road. Cross main road and go through gate opposite onto disused railway track on embankment with fields (L & R). Continue **SO** to main road. (**#7 & TR Link #2**)

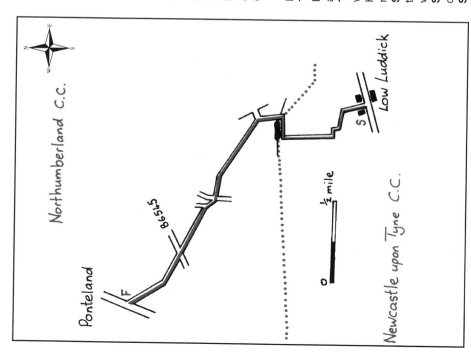

Northumberland C.C.

Ponteland

B6545

Low Luddick

Newcastle upon Tyne C.C.

0   ½ mile

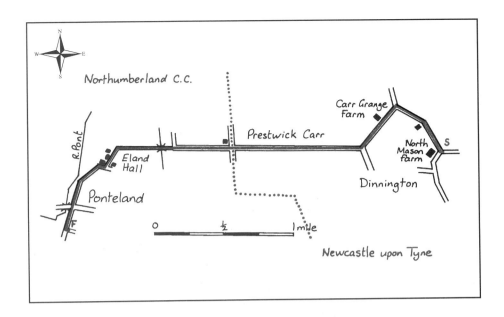

Link Route 2. Double Duck
Dinnington to Ponteland

Distance:	**3.5 miles (5.6 Km.)**
Level:	**Easy**
Maps:	**Ordnance Survey Pathfinder 536 'Whitley Bay'; 535 'Ponteland'.**
Facilities:	**None on route.**

Introduction
This route links Route 4 'Hunter's Handicap' (page 23) with Route 7 'The Mekon' (page 35). It also joins Link Route 1 'Duck'.

It uses the remarkably straight Prestwick Carr which is nearly 2.5 miles long. This road passes a rifle range and you may hear gunshots or encounter red flags flying at either end. As long as you stay on the road you are in no danger from bullets but the uneven road surface can be just as dangerous. Close to Ponteland the route passes the picturesque duckpond at Eland Hall Farm.

Route Description
Where the track joins the main road at 'North Mason Farm' in Dinnington **(#4) TR** and follow the road past farm (L). Take the next **TL** past 'Carr Grange Farm' (R) and **SO** to fork in road. Watch out for traffic from the L and **TR** into 'Prestwick Carr' signposted 'Road Unsuitable for Motors'. Go **SO** at crossroads. At the sharp bend to the R go **SO** onto narrow track, over bridge and downhill to gate. Go through gate onto wide grassy track, continue **SO** and join a gravel track. Follow this track round to **L** towards farm buildings (R). Through gate **TL** onto tarmac surface past duckpond (R). Follow the road round to **L** and **R** between houses then go downhill bearing to **L** past new estate (L) and 'River Pont' (R). Continue **SO** to traffic lights in centre of Ponteland. **SO** across main road onto B6323 signposted 'Darras Hall Estate 1/2'. 'Ponteland Sports Centre' is 150 metres down this road on the **L. (#7 & Link #1)**

57

Link Route 3. Spring Well
Cycle Tunnel to Dunkirk Farm via Bowes Railway

Distance: 7.6 miles (12.2 Km.)

Level: Medium

Maps: Ordnance Survey Pathfinder 562 'Washington & Chester-le-Street'; 549 'Newcastle upon Tyne'

Facilities: Toilets at Bowes Museum and Monkton Stadium. Various pubs on route.

Introduction

This route links three circuits south of the Tyne: Route 3 'The Early Bath' (page 19), Route 8 'Walk Away Renee' (page 39) and Route 10 'Derailed or Derailleur' (page 47). In addition via Link Route 4 'Well Sprung' (page 60) it connects with Route 5 'Up and Under' (page 27).

Route Description

From the tunnel (#3) head for the cone shaped ventilator shaft. **TR** at the road and follow this road **L** to roundabout. **TR** signposted 'Ring Road Hebburn B1297'. **SO** past 'Rolling Mill' and 'Jarrow Lad' public houses. As this road bears to R **TL** into 'Kings Court' industrial estate. Go **SO** under railway bridge onto cycleway ahead. Continue **SO** through barrier, across road (A185) onto cycleway opposite. **SO** through barriers, past works (R) and take **R** fork in path. **SO** to barrier and T junction with road. **TR** and go **SO** past 'The Lord Nelson' public house (R). Bear **L** on 'Monkton Lane' and continue **SO** to end of street. Through barrier **TR** onto gravel track. **TR** at crossroads of tracks and **TL** at T junction ahead. **TR** at fork in paths and go **SO** to join road. **TR** along road to T junction. **TR** then immediately **TL** onto tarmac path under power lines. Follow this path **L** then **TR**. Cycle round the pond (L) and go **SO** to railway cutting. **TL** and cross rough ground close to railway embankment (R). At the bridge **TR** onto disused mineral line and cross bridge. Contine **SO** across road and under main road. Go **SO** across next main road to

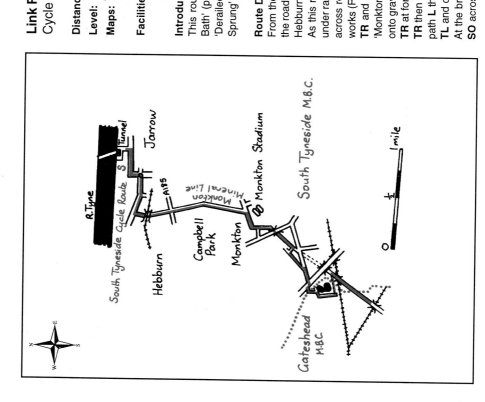

58

'Public Bridle Path' opposite. Go **SO** across next road and continue uphill. **(TR #8)** Pass the 'Bowes Railway Museum' (L) into the car park. Leave at the gate and **TL** onto road. After 100 metres **TR** onto path signposted 'Leam Lane 3/4'. At the end bear **R** and follow track diagonally across field. *Please note from the road to this corner is footpath. **TL** here onto track and **SO** to join undulating gravel track. Follow this to railway (R) and after 150 metres cross track at 'The Waggon Inn' public house (R). **SO** track ahead and take **R** fork in path. Bear to **R** and then steeply downhill to road. Cross road with 'Lambton Arms' public house (R) to steep downhill track opposite. At bottom follow track to **L** then **R**, **SO** past pond (R) to join disused railway line to **R** of bridge. **TR** downhill for 100 metres to 'Dunkirk' farm. (#10)

Cycle Routes in South Tyneside

South Tyneside Council have developed several cycle routes and others are currently being developed. Those already available are:

South Tyneside Cycle Route - from the Tyne pedestrian tunnel to the Keelman's Way via Hebburn Riverside Cycleway.

The River Don Route - starts near the historic St Paul's Church and Bede Monastery Museum and follows the river through the Primrose Nature Reserve to Mill Dene Town Farm.

Monkton Mineral Line - a mostly off road link from the South Tyne Cycleway to the Bowes Railway Path.

Tilesheds Nature Reserve - within this recreational site are 1.5 miles of dedicated bridleway including a circular route of 1 mile.

There is also a link route from East Boldon Station to Lizard Lane and the Coast Road which is off road, but not all surfaced, nearly all the way. For further information including free leaflets and a map showing cycle routes in South Tyneside contact:

South Tyneside MBC, Town Hall & Civic Offices, Westoe Road,
South Shields, NE33 2RL.
Telephone (0191) 427 1717

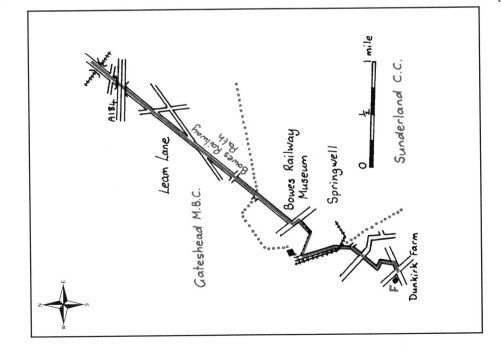

Link Route 4. Well Sprung

Cycle Tunnel to Stephenson Railway Museum

Distance:	3.0 miles (4.8 Km.)
Level:	Easy
Maps:	**Ordnance Survey Pathfinder 549 'Newcastle upon Tyne'**
Facilities:	**Pubs and shops near Tyne Tunnel.**

Introduction

This route links Route 3 'The Early Bath' (page 19) with Route 5 'Up and Under' (page 27). However, in conjunction with Link Route 3 'Spring Well' (page 57), it forms a strategic north-south link making several interesting combinations possible.

Route Description

Leave pedestrian tunnel uphill to T junction with main road. (#3) **TR** and continue until road bears **L** to roundabout. At this point **TR** across road onto lane and then **TL** onto shared pedestrian/cycleway. **SO** past 'Duke of Wellington' public house (R) into 'Gallant Terrace' and go up this street. At the top **SO** to join shared path then **TR** alongside main road (L). Continue **SO** at first roundabout. Just before the next roundabout **TL** to cross dual carriageway at the safe crossing place.

SO short path and bear **L** onto road. At 'Percy Main Cricket Club' (R) **TR** onto 'St John's Green'. As this street bears R go **SO** through gate onto path. **SO** through barrier and under bridge at end.

Bear **R** at 'The Percy Arms' (L) staying on the path by the road. After about 150 metres bear **R** then **L** at bushes and go **SO** under bridge to long straight cycleway ahead with railway line (L). Continue **SO** this track, under another bridge, to T junction with road. **TL** and 100 metres along the road **TL** into museum car park and finish. (#5)

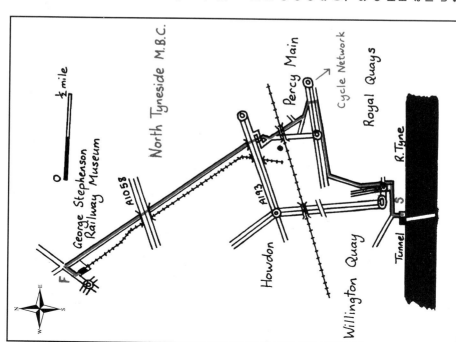

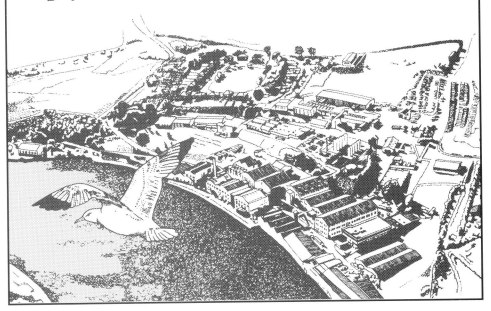

NOTES